My Past

My Past

Reminiscences of the Courts of Austria and
Bavaria; Together with the true story
of the events leading up to the tragic death
of Rudolph, Crown Prince of Austria

Marie Larisch

(Countess Marie Wallersee-Larisch)

With an introduction by
John Van der Kiste

A & F Reprints

First published by Eveleigh Nash, London and Putnam, New York 1913
This edition published by A & F 2019

Introduction © 2019 John Van der Kiste

A & F Publications,
South Brent, Devon, England, UK, TQ10 9AS

Typeset 11pt Century

ISBN 9781096092582

Printed by KDP

To

MY FRIEND
MAUDE MARY CHESTER FFOULKES

WHO HAS ASSISTED ME
TO PREPARE MY BOOK FOR PUBLICATION

1

CONTENTS

My father, Duke Ludwig of Bavaria · Five fair sisters · A morganatic marriage · My mother · The castle of Garatshausen · The Empress Elizabeth's visit · An Imperial retinue · I see my beautiful aunt for the first time · Her wonderful air · A daughter of sun and fire · Her fascination · I wander in the garden and climb a tree · Day-dreams · Why did the Empress weep? · My hiding place is discovered · "Did you see me cry?" · "Aunt Cissi" talks to me · What she wanted to know · The beginning of the tangled web · Farewell · A present for a wise little girl · We go to Rome · An audience with the Pope · A religious examination · How I met Richard Wagner · He is mistaken for Duke Ludwig's tailor · "Let him wait" · I am reprimanded for my masquerade

We visit Vienna · The black silk dress · Macassar oil · Our Bavarian maid · "No skating in August" · The grub becomes a butterfly · A ride in the Prater · A family dinner – The Crown Prince Rudolph · Hungry at the Opera · We return to Munich · Marriage projects · King Ludwig vetoes a Bismarck marriage – Feldafing · A Royal family · My aunt's confidences · A fairy tale

CHAPTER V: A ROYAL INVASION OF ENGLAND

CHAPTER VI: INDISCRETIONS AND ECCENTRICITIES

INTRODUCTION

In 1913, the last year of the old European order before the outbreak of the First World War and the end of the three great empires, Countess Marie Larisch published her memoirs, *My Past*. Her past had indeed been a notorious one, including above all a sordid role in the tragedy of Mayerling, when Crown Prince Rudolph of Austria-Hungary shot dead his mistress Mary Vetsera and then himself in January 1889.

Born in Augsburg, Bavaria, on 24 February 1858, she was the illegitimate daughter of actress Henriette Mendel (1833-91) and Ludwig Wilhelm, Duke in Bavaria (1831-1920), eldest son of Duke Maximilian Joseph in Bavaria (1808-88) and Princess Ludovika of Bavaria (1808-92), and brother of Elizabeth, Empress of Austria (1837-98). In 1859 her father renounced his rights as the firstborn son of the ducal family, her mother was created *Freifrau* (Baroness) *von Wallersee* two months later, and they married morganatically. Marie also thus became *Freiin* (also Baroness) *von Wallersee.* Partly because of her skills on horseback, she became close to her aunt the Empress, who arranged a marriage between Marie and Count Georg Larisch of Moennich, Baron of Ellgoth and Karwin (1855-1928).

The wedding took place on 20 October 1877 and Marie had five children, Franz-Joseph Ludwig Georg Maria, Count Larisch of Moennich, Baron of Ellgoth and Karwin (1878–1937); Marie Valerie (1879–1915); Marie Henriette (1884–1907); Georg (1886–1909); and Friedrich Karl (1894–1929). The first two were fathered by the Count, but the paternity of the three younger was uncertain. She was noted for her extravagance, and her cousin Crown Prince Rudolph helped to finance the lifestyle she demanded that was beyond the limited means of her husband.

Because she was continually indebted to the heir to the throne, she was obliged to procure certain favours for him, which included acting as a go-between with any young woman who took his fancy.

According to Joan Haslip (*The Lonely Empress: A Biography of Elizabeth of Austria*, 1965), Marie Larisch's motives were hard to understand. She was probably once in love with Rudolph, had been his mistress and hoped to be his wife. (As his own parents, Empress Elizabeth and Emperor Francis Joseph, were first cousins, such consanguinity would have presented no difficulty.) Once she realised that this was not going to happen, she accepted the role of friend and confidante, ready to pander to his wishes. She was known to be quite amoral and saw no harm in introducing him to Mary Vetsera, a flighty girl of seventeen, whom he would not fail to ruin. Mary came from a notorious family, and her mother, Baroness Helene Vetsera, was rumoured to have had an extra-marital liaison with the Emperor some eighteen years previously. It was not very likely, but yet not completely impossible, that Mary was the Crown Prince's half-sister.

After the deaths of the young couple at Mayerling, a letter was found in the Crown Prince's personal effects, mentioning sums of money having been paid by him to Marie Larisch for services rendered. These included introducing Mary to him, accompanying her on her secret visits to his apartments in the Hofburg, and facilitating their assignations when they met in rooms owned by a friend of the Crown Prince in Vienna. This letter was sufficient evidence alone to confirm Marie's responsibility in the tragedy that had shaken the Habsburg dynasty to its foundations. It destroyed her relationship with the Empress and the rest of the imperial family, and from that moment on she was *persona non grata* in Viennese society.

She moved to Bavaria, and her marriage to the Count broke down shortly afterwards. They were divorced in December 1896, and five months later she married the musician Otto Brucks (1854–1914). They had one child, a son Otto (1899-1977). Her husband had previously been a famous opera singer, but the marriage brought a sudden end to his career, for he was no longer offered any engagements as he was the husband of one of Europe's notorious outcasts, and he became an alcoholic.

Anxious to exploit such resources she still had, she turned to writing about her association with the imperial house for any editors who would use her work. The family paid her handsomely not to sell her memoirs, but she realised there was more money to be made in breaking than honouring any such contract, and to quote the Duke of Wellington's immortal dictum, 'publish and be damned'. The first of several books of which she was nominally the author was *My Past,* ghostwritten by Maude Mary Chester Ffoulkes (1871-1949). *Secrets of a Royal House* followed in 1934, and *My Royal Relatives* two years later. All of them make interesting reading, but are not wholly reliable as sources of historical information. Self-serving to the last, her aim was not only to make money and exploit her imperial past, but also exculpate her from blame or responsibility for the suicide of the cousin who was to have become Emperor of Austria. She was more successful in the first aim than the second.

As she recounts in the present work:

> There have been many accounts written of the drama of Mayerling. Various people have asserted that they alone know the truth. So-called eye-witnesses have given their versions of the affair, and a tissue of lies has been woven around me in connection with the deaths of my cousin, the Crown Prince Rudolph of Austria, and the Baroness Mary Vetsera. Hitherto I have not refuted the slanders circulated about me, as I deemed them unworthy of notice. But as one of my sons [*Georg, her second*] shot himself on account of what he read in one of the lying books, and my daughters' lives have been embittered by hearing so much that is untrue regarding the part I played in the drama, I have made up my mind to speak after a silence of twenty-four years and acquaint the world with the truth of what really happened before and after the tragedy of Mayerling (Chapter IX, pp.121-2).

At some point around this time she met the young poet T.S. Eliot. He immortalised her in one of the early stanzas of *The Waste Land* (1922):

And when we were children, staying at the archduke's,
My cousin's, he took me out on a sled,
And I was frightened. He said, Marie,
Marie, hold on tight. And down we went.
In the mountains, there you feel free.

To her credit, in her homeland's hour of need during the First World War, she underwent six months of training as a nurse and served as a Red Cross supervisor in charge of hospital trains. When peace came in 1918, all royalties were deposed if not sent into exile (if not worse), and members of the aristocracy were considered 'the enemy'. Munich had fallen under control of the Workers and Solders Council, and to quote her own words, 'the Red Terror grasped Bavaria in its bloody claw'. When required to show her papers identifying her as a member of the royal Wittelsbach family to an official, she was able to obtain a passport that described her as 'Marie Wallersee, medical assistant and nurse'. For a while she worked as a doctor's assistant. After leaving Munich for Berlin she became a servant, with duties including cooking and washing dishes, laundry and floors, but was paid much less than the legal minimum wage. Her son Otto worked hard to save enough funds to bring her back to Munich.

Next, a unique opportunity opened for her. The motion picture industry, then in its infancy, was ready to exploit the unquenchable thirst for books, magazine articles and anything to do with the more mysterious aspects of the last but one Emperor and Empress's family. A company named Indra Films came to Munich to make a picture based on Crown Prince Rudolph and the Mayerling episode. She visited the owner, Rolf Raffe, and offered to place her expertise and experience as an eye-witness to contemporary events at his disposal. He accordingly hired her as a consultant, and she nominally wrote the screenplay, as well as acting as co-director, her knowledge of the old imperial court proving invaluable. The resulting production, *Crown Prince Rudolf, or The Secret of Mayerling*, was an immediate success.

Inevitably, surviving Archdukes and Archduchesses were angered by her participation in this just as much as they had been by her book, but she had effectively been expelled from the family for over thirty years, and despite any agreements made with members of the now dethroned imperial house, no longer considered herself under any obligation. It was unofficially banned in Vienna in deference to the wishes of Rudolf's only legitimate daughter, Archduchess Elisabeth, on the grounds that it 'contradict[ed] decency and good manners to film occurrences from private life'.

Unabashed, Marie and Raffe collaborated on two more films. She was partly responsible for the screenplay of *Silence at Lake Starnberg*, based around the death of King Ludwig II of Bavaria, and with her family connections she obtained permission for Raffe to film part at the King's private residence, Schloss Herrenchiemsee. The last was a production about the murder of Empress Elizabeth. Now aged sixty-three, she was chosen to play herself as a woman of thirty on-screen, and also to help coach the young actress portraying the Empress as effectively as possible. Despite the family's intense disapproval of anything associated with Marie, it was said that the Empress's elder daughter, Archduchess Gisela, was persuaded to see the film, and was in tears as she was so moved by the star's resemblance to her mother. Succeeding generations have no chance of passing their own judgment. Only a thirty-second fragment of the film, showing the deathbed scene, is known to survive (see p.118).

After this celluloid trilogy, Marie was thrown back on her own resources. She had received alimony from her first ex-husband, who was still alive, but post-war hyperinflation in Germany ar rendered any sums paid almost worthless. An article was published in the American press, suggesting that the widowed Countess was prepared to marry anyone who would pay her and her son their fare to the United States. An offer was made to her to manage a sanitorium in the United States owned by a naturopath, William H. Meyers (1859-?) and his business partner, and on 2 September 1924 she married him. They settled in Florida, but it was a very brief union. Within two years she had fled the marital home to escape from his beatings, and gone to

New Jersey to work as a housemaid. They were divorced in 1928 and she returned to Germany a year later.

Two more books appeared under her name, *Secrets of a Royal House* (1934) and *My Royal Relatives* (1936). Count Larisch died in 1928, and her son inherited the title as well as presumably any estate still left to the family. Apart from royalties accruing from her last two books, he was probably her sole means of support during her declining years. All but forgotten by the world at large, she died on 4 July 1940, aged eighty-two, at Augsburg and was buried in the Ostfriedhof, the 'Eastern Cemetery' in Munich.

So is *My Past* a valuable historical memoir, or an exercise in muck-raking with two eyes firmly focused on the publisher's advance and the royalties – or somewhere in between? If some of it reads as if it is all too strange to be true, it must be remembered that the Habsburgs and the Wittelsbachs had their share of eccentrics; as the author said, the former were 'a House conspicuous for the number of its members who have done the maddest things'. One of the most far-sighted, Crown Prince Rudolf's successor as heir to the imperial throne Archduke Francis Ferdinand, too many of his close relatives had been victims of inbreeding on an alarming scale. Some of what she (and Ffoulkes) wrote carries the ring of truth, although there is no doubt that the Countess considered herself grossly maligned, and chose to rewrite history to some extent in order to try and rehabilitate herself.

Let us quote from the judgments of experts through the ages. Egon Caesar Conte Corti, in *Elizabeth, Empress of Austria* (1936), states that it 'contains much romancing, and is such a blend of truth and fiction, seasoned with malicious insinuations, that ... it cannot be used as a historical source'. Haslip's more recent life of the Empress referred to above calls the memoirs 'both vindictive and inaccurate', but concedes that 'they nevertheless give a true picture of Elizabeth's character'. Two more recent writers, Greg King and Penny Wilson, in *Twilight of Empire: The Tragedy at Mayerling and the End of the Habsburgs* (2017), call the book 'an entertaining if highly questionable rendering of [Marie's] involvement in the Mayerling affair'.

My Past was published in 1913 in Britain by Eveleigh Nash, and in America by Putnam. An advertisement in *The Times* on 20 May 1913, which proclaimed '3 editions in 10 days', included a message from the publisher:

> Attempts have been made by certain critics to misrepresent the character of the Countess Marie Larisch's memoirs, and to minimize their manifest importance. Mr Nash has the satisfaction of stating that the public has treated these attacks with the contempt they deserve, for he has received letters from all parts of the country congratulating him on publishing a book so fearlessly honest, and so clearly ringing with truth. No volume is at present being so widely read, and it is the topic of conversation in every capital in Europe.

Although the text is the same in both editions, there are marked differences. The British edition has neither chapter titles nor illustrations (while the American has twenty-two of the latter), and I am assuming my copy is probably a second edition closely following on the first, as it includes 'A reply to my critics' at the front. There are also minor differences in the wording of her dedication to Mary Maude Chester Ffoulkes (the one used in this volume follows the British edition), the order of information included in the preliminary pages, and minor differences in punctuation, italicisation, hyphenation and conjoining of words. For example, I have preferred the British edition's 'black silk' to the American's 'blacksilk', but otherwise kept editing to the bare minimum. A few footnotes have been expanded, updated and added as necessary; the book was written and first published while her father and a couple of her aunts, as well as her uncle Emperor Francis Joseph, were still alive. The latter remains a hyphenated 'Francis-Joseph' as per the original book, although I have taken the liberty of preferring the more popular spelling of 'Mayerling' to her 'Meyerling'. I have omitted the index, added different illustrations to the American version, and a genealogical table.

John Van der Kiste

A REPLY TO MY CRITICS

When *My Past* was published on May 1st, 1913, I was in London, and nearly every important newspaper reviewed my book at considerable length.

With the exception of the *Daily Mail*,* a morning journal noted for the nature of its news, I was greatly impressed by the courtesy and fairness of the criticisms — even those in which the reviewers accepted some of my statements with reserve. It did not surprise me that my story of the steel box was regarded by certain critics as a tale that might have been taken from the pages of a lurid melodrama, or that what I had to record about the Crown Prince Rudolph and Hungary should have seemed to some minds incredible.

I now take this opportunity of stating that I never affirmed that the Crown Prince was plotting for the throne of Hungary. I only believe from all I heard, and from what I knew of Rudolph, that he was involved in a conspiracy to make him king. Nothing is easier than to ridicule the idea, but I think it is always well for normal people not to judge from their own standpoints those who suffer from disordered minds. Rudolph was abnormal, and he belonged to a House conspicuous for the number of its members who have done the maddest things.

---

* In its notice of my book the *Daily Mail* implied that it knew more about the Austrian Imperial Family than I did, and in the course of its comments, which included a sneer at my dead mother, it informed its readers that the Archduke John of Tuscany was a brother of the Crown Prince Rudolph, the only son of the Emperor Francis Joseph.

The Crown Prince died only forty-one years after the Hungarian revolution of 1848, and at a time when there was lingering bitterness between the sister kingdoms. Hence the conjecture that Rudolph dallied with an invitation to become king is not so improbable as it may seem, for Francis Joseph's popularity in Hungary was by no means widespread in those days. Had Rudolph been crowned at Budapest, he would have freed himself from certain restrictions imposed upon him as heir to the Austrian throne, and might have married a woman even of the rank of the Baroness Mary Vetsera had he been able to get his union with Stephanie annulled.

With regard to the steel box, I can only affirm that the Crown Prince handed it to me in the manner I have described, and later I delivered it to the Archduke John in circumstances which I know full well read like the invention of some romantic writer, I described the casket, which was covered with cloth, as being made of steel, because it weighed heavily, and Rudolph said that it was so, and not because I desired to emulate those purveyors of melodrama whose stage villains are so frequently the possessors of a steel box when documents play a part in the plot.

I have told the truth; I had nothing to gain by invention or distortion of facts. I wrote my book because I desired to do so, and not because I was tempted by money, or inspired by malice, to disclose what I knew.

ILLUSTRATIONS

Between pages 106 and 119

CHAPTER I
A ROMANTIC CHILDHOOD

*My father, Duke Ludwig of Bavaria - Five fair sisters –
A morganatic marriage – My mother - The castle of Garatshausen -
The Empress Elizabeth's visit - An Imperial retinue - I see my
beautiful aunt for the first time - Her wonderful hair - A daughter of
sun and fire - Her fascination - I wander in the garden and climb a
tree - Day-dreams - Why did the Empress weep? – My hiding place
is discovered - "Did you see me cry?" - "Aunt Cissi" talks to me -
What she wanted to know - The beginning of the tangled web -
Farewell – A present for a wise little girl - We go to Rome - An
audience with the Pope – A religious examination - How I met
Richard Wagner - He is mistaken for Duke Ludwig's tailor - "Let
him wait" - I am reprimanded for my masquerade*

My father, Duke Ludwig of Bavaria, who is now in his eighty-
second year,* is the brother of those five fair sisters, Elizabeth
Empress of Austria, Marie-Sophie (Sophia) ex-queen of Naples,
Sophie-Charlotte Duchesse d'Alençon, Mathilde Princess Trani,
and Hélène Princess Thurn and Taxis. On May 28, 1859, after
having previously renounced his rights as eldest son of the Duke
of Bavaria, he contracted a morganatic marriage with Henrietta
Mendel, a beautiful young actress who was created Baroness von
Wallersee, and I was their only child. The Ducal family received
my mother quite as one of themselves, and she was delighted to
leave the stage, which she frankly detested. She was not one of
those women who sacrifice fame for love and live unhappily ever
afterwards; she suffered from no illusions regarding her ability as
an actress, and was well aware that the secret of her popularity
lay in her pretty face and engaging manner.

* He died in 1920, aged eighty-nine.

I was born at Augsburg near Munich, where my father commanded the 4th Regiment of Light Horse. We lived in a large house in the town and every summer we spent a few months in the mountains. I was brought up just like a boy, for when I was three years old and my mother took me in her carriage to see the soldiers, papa's great amusement consisted in lifting me up by the scruff of the neck on to his horse, and galloping away with me seated in front of him. Thus my early familiarity with horses made me heedless of danger, and at five years of age I used to ride a spirited pony.

I was educated at home and hated all of my many excellent and long-suffering governesses. I learned to fence and to ride six horses a day, and I was certainly to all intents and purposes a very boyish girl. After the war of 1866 we went to live in Munich, first at a house in the town, and then at my father's own palace; there more teachers worried me and were worried by me, but I succeeded in acquiring a fair knowledge of Latin.

About this time my father's health made it imperative for him to leave the Army, but the internal trouble from which he suffered did not prevent him from enjoying his ordinary pursuits. We often went to our castle of Garatshausen, which was close to my grandparents' castle of Possenhofen on the Lake of Starnberg, and one day my father told us that he had lent Garatshausen for six weeks to his sister the Empress Elizabeth, who wanted to bring the baby Archduchess Valérie from Vienna, for a change of air. I was all excitement to see the aunt about whom I had heard so much, and, child though I was, I shall never forget my first meeting with the fascinating, enigmatic woman who was destined to exercise such a powerful influence on my life.

It was summer, and Garatshausen looked its loveliest. We had temporarily removed to a little house nearby, but on the day of the Empress's arrival we awaited her in the cool vestibule of the castle. Her trusted doctor, Wiederhofer, and Mrs. Throgmorton, Valérie's devoted English nurse, arrived in advance, and I remember how interested I was to see the carriages which contained the Imperial entourage, for Elizabeth travelled with a great retinue of servants of all grades.

An hour passed and then a carriage with magnificent horses drew up. A lady alighted from it and entered the hall. She kissed my mother and my father affectionately, then she turned to where I was standing and kissed me, exclaiming as she did so in that half-mocking tone so peculiar to her, "Oh, what a lanky little girl!"

I gazed at her spellbound, for with some curious intuition I already felt her influence over me, and I thought that here was a Fairy Queen who had come straight from the realms of Romance, having temporarily discarded her gauzy wings and shimmering robes for a green and black plaid burnous, grey hat, and a long-trained black dress.

Elizabeth seemed amused and pleased by my childish admiration, and, after kissing us all again, went to her apartments, and we saw her no more that day. I could talk of nothing else but her, and my parents had to pacify me by saying that I should be sure to see "Aunt Cissi" again very soon, as she had expressed a wish for me to play with little Valérie during their stay at Garatshausen.

I was not disappointed; next morning the Empress sent for me, and I was all impatience to go to her.

I was more than ever enraptured when I saw her again. Elizabeth was sitting at breakfast, whilst her hairdresser arranged her hair. She was too beautiful for words, at least I thought so, and indeed the Empress, then in the height of her beauty, was a lovely picture. A négligee of exquisite lace enveloped her slender figure, and her wonderful hair, which I saw for the first time unbound, flowed around her in heavy chestnut waves. Her inscrutable eyes were of a deep amber flecked with gold, and the searching daylight discovered no flaw in her. Elizabeth seemed a daughter of sun and fire as she sat there in the golden glow which intensified her loveliness and her strange ethereal look.

I soon knew the reason of my summons. I was to play with Valérie in the afternoon. Aunt Cissi then said she was going to ride, and I was dismissed. The longed-for interview was over, and I went away a slave to her fascination and beauty. It was quite impossible for me to go home. I wanted to be alone, so I wandered into the gardens, fished for crayfish in the ponds, and when I tired of this hitherto absorbing pastime I climbed up a tree, took off my wet stockings, which I hung on a branch to dry, and resumed my day-dreams about the Empress.

I remembered all I had heard about her, and being a precocious child I also recollected that papa had sometimes said that "Cissi" was not too happy. "But it can't be true, she can't be unhappy," I thought, as I reviewed the scene of the morning, for the splendour and state which surrounded my aunt as Empress of Austria had greatly impressed me.

Suddenly I heard the sound of approaching footsteps, and peering from my leafy screen I nearly fell out of the tree when I recognised the Empress, who had apparently given up the idea of riding, and was walking quite unattended. Although the sunlight heightened Elizabeth's beauty she was afraid of its effects, and always wore a curious blue shade fixed on her hat as a protection from sunburn and freckles, and in the evening she invariably carried a fan to shield her face.

Elizabeth came slowly to my tree, under which was a stone seat. She sat down, clasped her hands in a despairing kind of way, and began to cry silently. I could see that she was greatly distressed, for her face wore a hopeless expression, and occasionally a sob shook her. She then wept unrestrainedly, and at last I wondered whether I dared attempt to comfort her. I bent down, and as the leaves rustled with my sudden movement, the Empress looked up and saw me. She quickly regained her composure and said sweetly:

"What are you doing in that tree, Marie?"

"I was getting my stockings dry, Aunt Cissi," I replied shamefacedly.

"Why, what have you been doing?"

"Fishing for crayfish ... I'm very, very dirty," I stammered.

"Come down from the tree, Marie," said my aunt. "I want to talk to you."

I dared not disobey, so most unwillingly I slid down, and stood before my aunt, barelegged, covered with streaks of green mould, and holding my soaking, sand-filled stockings in my hand. Oh, why couldn't I be a pretty little girl?" I thought bitterly. "Why was I fated to see the Empress in such unfavourable circumstances?" Yesterday she had called me a "lanky" child. What must I look like now? In utter self-abasement I fidgeted from one foot to the other, waiting for her to speak.

"Marie," she said, looking at me with beautiful, tear-drenched eyes, "answer at once. Did you see me cry?"

"Yes, Aunt Cissi."

"Why do you think I was crying?"

"I don't know," I said with perfect truth, for I could not imagine what on earth could move an Empress to tears. I did not know that her Imperial crown was weighted with sorrow, and that its jewels were but sharp thorns; I did not dream that her noble nature, chilled in the early days of what might have been an ideal union, was becoming warped, and that she was schooling herself to practise that reticence and repression which later was to have disastrous results for those who came within her influence.

"Well, I'll tell you the reason why I am so miserable; come beside me ... there ..." - as I sat down timidly and tried to conceal my hateful legs - "don't be afraid. Valérie was ill during the night, and I was anxious, so that is why I cried."

It occurred to me that my aunt had not seemed disturbed about my cousin's health when I saw her at breakfast, but I merely answered:

"Oh, Valérie will be all right soon, Aunt Cissi."

"How do you know, and why do you say so?"

"Because," I said, with great confidence in the truth of my statement, "because I'll have a Novena for her, and that always helps."

The Empress did not speak; she seemed deep in thought. She looked at me from time to time and smiled strangely; then she took my dirty, hot little hand in hers and said, "Well, Marie, we must not sit here any longer; let us go back to the castle." My aunt still held my hand, and we walked through the charming gardens in silence.

It was a delightful morning, and Garatshausen with its four towers stood out sharply against a background of azure sky; a refreshing wind came from the distant mountains, and, as I timidly glanced at Elizabeth, I saw that she looked quite herself again. Just as the entrance to the castle came in sight, she stopped, looked at me with eyes which seemed to search my inmost thoughts, and said:

"Now, I want to know, Marie, whether you can hold your tongue, or are you a silly chatterbox who tells everything?"

I was rather offended, and said sulkily, but with a great show of dignity, "I am *not* a chatterbox, Aunt Cissi. And of course I can hold my tongue."

The Empress smiled. "Very well, then, Marie, prove it to me, and don't tell a soul that you saw me crying ... I shall soon know if you are really a wise child."

My afternoon with little Valérie seemed somewhat dull after my exciting morning, and I did not say that I had spent part of it with my aunt when mamma scolded me for my long absence. Something told me that the Empress would not mention our meeting, and a romantic wish to be trusted by her kept me silent. Looking with regret on the years that are past, I am tempted to wish that I had been a chatterbox, for although my aunt's affection for me was to surround me later with all that the average woman desires, the beginning of my destiny dates from that summer day, when Elizabeth Empress of Austria asked me whether I always told *everything* I knew.

During the weeks which passed, my aunt did not appear to remember our conversation, for, she never referred to it when I happened to be alone with her. I enjoyed every day of that wonderful visit, and I idolised Valérie, who was a sweet child. Mrs. Throgmorton used to afford me endless delight, for she would emulate the antics of a dancing dervish in order to amuse the little Archduchess, and the contrast between her usual air of importance and her lack of dignity when she danced was extremely funny.

Elizabeth loved Garatshausen, and when the time came for her return to Vienna she took leave of my parents with tears in her eyes. We all stood in the marble vestibule where we had awaited her arrival, and I thought she looked lovelier than ever in her white dress and white hat with plumes that swept the burnished chestnut of her hair.

Valérie was a picture in white and mauve, and when the Empress had given my mother another affectionate embrace, she came to where I was standing, and pressed a little velvet case into my hand, saying as she did so, "Here is a souvenir from Valérie *for a wise little girl.*"

Then she went away; the carriage disappeared in a cloud of dust, and only the faint sounds of wheels in the distance served to remind us of our beautiful relation. I did not open the little case until I was alone. Then I pressed the spring and found a gold locket with the initials of Marie Valérie glittering in rubies and emeralds. Inside was a miniature of the child, and a date which was at first meaningless, until a sudden enlightenment told me it was a reminder of that day in the gardens of Garatshausen. So the Empress had not forgotten after all.

When we returned to Munich, life went on as usual and some years passed before I saw my aunt again. But absence in no way made her less of a heroine to me, and I endeavoured to excel in those things which I knew appealed to her. Therefore I became a good horsewoman, able to remain in the saddle for hours without being fatigued. I fenced, I walked, I was a fair shot, I always remembered that I must not talk at random, and thus I tried to qualify myself for the approval of the Empress.

When I was twelve years old my father was ordered to Italy by his doctors, so we went to Rome accompanied by our Bavarian medical adviser, a big stout man with an astonishing capacity for eating. Papa used to ascribe many of his own minor ailments to his early education in Saxony, where in the days of his youth he gravitated between Dresden and the castle of Pillnitz. He was wont to observe that the dullness and depression of Dresden gave him a perpetual headache and that the unsavoury food at Pillnitz gave him a perpetual stomach-ache, and probably served to lay the foundation of his future digestive troubles.

When we arrived at Rome we naturally wished, as good Catholics, to be received by the Holy Father, and as a preliminary we visited Cardinal Antonelli, who knew my religious instructor, a Munich priest, very well.

Pius IX gave us a special audience, and I wore the black silk dress and black veil which are *de rigueur* on these occasions. I wanted to laugh because I thought I looked absolutely freakish in my grown-up gown; in fact, we all looked incongruous. Mamma wore black, papa was in uniform, and the Bavarian doctor sported an archaic tall hat. Papa kept telling us what we must do when we saw the Pope. "Kneel, kneel," he repeated at intervals, but when the crucial moment arrived and we all knelt before his Holiness, the doctor's hat slipped from his hands and rolled at a rapidly increasing speed over the polished floor. This did away with all feelings of restraint, for the Pope laughed and asked us to come into his private room and talk to him. Pius IX was most friendly, and took special notice of me. "I should like to have a talk with this little lady," he observed. "Will you send her to see me to-morrow morning?"

My parents were much flattered by the Pontifical condescension, and the next day my governess and I went to the Vatican. The Pope examined me in religion, we conversed together in Latin, and at the conclusion of his questionings Pius smiled and asked:

"Well - were you very frightened?"

"No," said I, for the Pope, who was a tall, well-built man, had one of those "good" faces which inspire confidence and affection.

"Ah! I am glad to hear it," he said; "but, truthfully, which do you prefer - a religious examination or dancing? When I was young I am sure I should have said I liked dancing better than religion."

His eyes twinkled, he patted my hand reassuringly, and before I left gave me his picture and a beautiful medallion, accompanying the gifts with his special blessing.

The Pope was most kind to our family. He stood sponsor to the Queen of Naples' daughter, and when misfortune overtook my aunt and uncle they lived for many years in the Farnese Palace.

One of my most interesting experiences as a young girl was my first meeting with Richard Wagner, who, as is well known, owed his ultimate recognition as a genius to the kindness and patronage of Ludwig II. The King, who was very fond of papa, one day asked him whether his fiancée, my aunt Princess Sophie of Bavaria, could meet Wagner at our house. Papa, of course, assented, and a meeting was arranged, but owing to some contretemps everybody excepting myself was out when the great man arrived. I had devoted my solitude to ransacking my mother's wardrobe to "dress up," so when I had tried on her largest crinoline, her silk dress, and her hat and jacket, I seized a small green silk-fringed umbrella, and pirouetted complacently in front of the long mirror.

Suddenly the bell rang, and conjecturing the arrival was my governess, I made for the door, opened it, and came face to face with Wagner, although I did not then know who he was. I remember him so well as a little man with a big nose who said politely, in a broad Saxon accent, "Is it here that the Duke of Bavaria lives?" I bowed, and said gravely, "Please to come in."

Wagner seemed rather nervous, and no wonder, for I looked extraordinary in my huge crinoline, and clothes which were far too large for me; but perhaps he reflected, that as our family was famed for its eccentricities, he had chanced to meet one of the "odd" members, so he followed me meekly into the drawing-room, where I left him.

An hour passed, and when my governess returned I informed her that papa's tailor was sitting in the salon, but she merely replied, "Let him wait," and directed her energies to scolding me for dressing up and telling me to "get on with my lessons."

There was no sound from where Wagner sat possessing his soul in patience, but when my mother came back and I imparted the interesting news to her that "Papa's tailor was in the salon," she straightway went to see for herself and nearly expired when she recognised Richard Wagner. Mamma was really distressed to think that he had been treated in such an offhand manner, and was profusely apologetic. Wagner, however, was highly amused, and remarked, "Some one told me to wait, and I *have* waited, you see."

Soon afterwards my aunt arrived with her lady-in-waiting, and I believe a very pleasant interview took place. I was not allowed to renew my acquaintance with Wagner, and in the outer darkness of my schoolroom I writhed under the maternal anger, but I have a shrewd suspicion that it was the fact of my "dressing up" which annoyed my mother most, and that Wagner's long wait was as nothing compared to her creased gown and roughly handled crinoline.

CHAPTER II
MY AUNT, THE EMPRESS

We visit Vienna - The black silk dress - Macassar oil - Our Bavarian maid - "No skating in August" - The grub becomes a butterfly - A ride in the Prater - A family dinner – The Crown Prince Rudolph - Hungry at the Opera - We return to Munich - Marriage projects - King Ludwig vetoes a Bismarck marriage – Feldafing - A Royal family – My aunt's confidences - A fairy tale - "Le Chapeau de Paille" - Marie-Josepha's charm - Her kindness to me - The great "Du" - Cross questions and crooked answers - I incur the Emperor's anger - I visit King Ludwig – Lohengrin as it was not written - Toothache cures - We are overtaken by a storm - The fisherman's widow - "He will return" – A strangely fulfilled prediction - The lucky rainbow - Flowers for "the little singer"

When I was fourteen the Empress invited my parents to visit her at Vienna, and they were specially enjoined to bring me with them. I was delighted at the prospect of meeting my aunt again, and greatly elated at the idea of seeing Vienna, which I had heard described as being the most splendid city in Europe.

The "lanky little girl" was now a regular maypole, and mamma decided that this visit must seal the fate of the short frocks which I had hitherto worn. My parents were simple-minded people, with a great distaste for display, and my toilettes had always been designed for utility and not for beauty. It may interest girls with extravagant ideas to know that three gowns were considered ample for me to wear during my visit - one for travelling, one for walking, and a black silk dress for great occasions. I hated this black silk with a deep-rooted hatred, for it was far too old in style, and I remonstrated against wearing it. "Do not let me hear any more of this nonsense," said papa, when I appealed to him; "if the dress is old-looking, at any rate it's very elegant!" I had another grievance, as, for some unknown reason, I was fitted with heavy-soled hob-nailed mountain-boots, and not with the light *chaussures* which are so appropriate for town wear. "What shall I look like?" I thought despairingly. "Aunt Cissi will call me a Bavarian peasant, and everybody will laugh at me." But my troubles were not over. Papa always detested my fair hair, and insisted on plentiful applications of hair-oil, in the vain hope that it would result ultimately in my being transformed from a blonde to a brunette. He became quite obsessed with the idea when the Vienna visit was mooted, and my locks were smeared frequently with oil every day. "Be sure you don't forget to pack a plentiful supply," he commanded; so we travelled with a perfect cellarful of bottles of Macassar oil.

At last the eventful day came when we left Munich, and arrived late in the evening at Penzing, the station for Schönbrunn, whence a court carriage conveyed us to the castle, where we did not see anyone that night. I had a beautiful bedroom with a very large bed, over which hung a picture of a sinister-looking archduke whose expression struck fear into my heart lest I should encounter him as a ghost.

A dainty supper was served, but papa was firm about our not eating too much late at night. "We must all sleep well," he observed, "for Cissi will be certain to pay us an early visit."

Our maid was a sturdy Bavarian girl from the mountains, who spoke an almost unintelligible *patois*, and whose ignorance of the *convenances* always kept my mother in a fever of anxiety. She was a good creature, however, and the next morning she called me early, and commenced a vigorous and plentiful hair-oiling. She rubbed in the oil just as a groom rubs down a horse, and between her puffing and rubbing she kept on ejaculating that surely no more thoroughly oiled hair could be found in Vienna. She then hooked me into the odious silk dress, which was far too long for me; my feet were encased in the big boots, and, glistening with oil, I "clumped" heavily into the charming room where my parents were seated.

"Himmel!" cried mamma, "Marie will fall over her dress. Quick ... bring me some pins," and straightway my skirt was festooned to a more suitable length. Coffee was then served, and we were just enjoying breakfast, when the Bavarian maid rushed *sans cérémonie* into the room shouting: "The Empress is coming." Through the door of the salon we had a view of room after room communicating one with the other. Endless doors were opened; some one was coming nearer, and then I saw that it was my beautiful aunt.

We all advanced to meet her. I say "advanced," but the word only applies to my parents' method of progression. *I* had not reckoned with my boots, and the result was that I slid ungracefully forward, to be greeted with a charming smile, and the words, "Well, Marie, there's no skating at Schönbrunn in August!"

I felt that the Empress was staring at my strange attire, and I was not mistaken. Suddenly she burst into fits of uncontrollable laughter, and when her amusement had somewhat subsided, she turned to my mother, who was rather perplexed as to what had caused her such merriment, and said in a stifled voice: "Oh, Henrietta, *do* allow Marie to come with me to my dressing-room."

I walked with my aunt to her private apartments, where her hairdresser and maids were awaiting her. Elizabeth turned to one of them, and said, "Bring plenty of gowns and lingerie, for my niece must be supplied with a complete outfit at once." She then went to her dressing-room to have her hair dressed, and the maids came in and out with piles of lovely gowns, delicate underlinen, dainty corsets, and delightful shoes. I had never before seen such luxury; it almost took my breath away. I revelled in the cambric and lace which soon replaced my plainly trimmed undergarments; the satin corsets suited my straight young figure, and my feet now presented an appearance of which I need not be ashamed. Of course, the gowns required various alterations, but the Empress selected those most suitable to my age, and lavished her lovely clothes upon me with prodigal generosity.

When the selection of gowns was over, my aunt looked at me critically, and said: "Take the Baroness away and wash the oil out of her hair." To me she remarked: "Now, Marie, I shall leave you alone to-day; thank heaven you are more presentable. To-morrow I shall meet you in the riding-school; I want to see how you can ride." She kissed me, and I was delivered into the hands of a maid who spent two strenuous hours washing my hair; but at last the ordeal was over, and in my new garments, with my thick fair hair guiltless of oil, I was taken back to our apartments.

The Bavarian girl gave a hoarse gurgle of astonishment at my transformation; papa turned on his heel, after having surveyed me, with thoughts which were too deep for words, and mamma's slightly wounded feelings, which had been upset by her sister-in-law's lack of appreciation of Bavarian fashions, were only mollified when, later in the day, the pretty gowns and other delightful accessories were sent me with "Aunt Cissi's love."

The next morning we went to the riding-school, where the Empress proved herself a critical observer of my capabilities as a horsewoman. I was told to ride three or four different horses, which, by the way, were all possessed of "temperaments," and at the conclusion of my efforts Elizabeth expressed herself greatly pleased, and told me I should ride with her in the Prater on the morrow. She then bore me off to be fitted with a habit, and made me try the effect of a high hat on my fair hair. "Far too old," she said emphatically. "No, Marie - just now it suits me that you should look a child. A straw sailor hat will be the very thing, and, mind, you are not to let them braid your hair, I want it to fall loose below your waist. We'll have such a pleasant time, and I will show you ever so many things which you have never seen in Munich."

Oh, how I adored this radiant lady who seemed to love me and to be so interested in my welfare! I was not an emotional child, but every chord in my heart responded to her. She fascinated me and dominated my imagination, and, with her infinite tact, she gave me confidence in myself. Elizabeth was never then the Empress, she was the Aunt Cissi who seemed so understanding, and so completely in sympathy with me, that I would willingly have died for her.

"The least said about your appearance the better," observed my father, as I stood ready for his inspection. "Cissi has certainly strange ideas, and that is all that can be said in excuse for my daughter looking like a fair-haired French doll." Mamma was more tolerant. "Well, certainly Marie's habit and hat are a little unusual in our eyes," she admitted, "but the child looks elegant, and we cannot oppose Elizabeth's wishes."

We drove to the Prater in two carriages, the Empress and her lady-in-waiting occupying the first, and my parents and I in the second. We stopped at Elizabeth's little cottage, which was surrounded by a pretty garden like a secluded oasis in the thronged Prater. There horses were waiting; we lost no time in mounting, and were soon the cynosure of all eyes, for it was the fashionable hour for the Prater, and smart Vienna was very much in evidence.

I rode at the Empress's right hand. We were followed by her head-groom and two undergrooms, and I can quite recall the sensation which the sight of Elizabeth created on that glorious August afternoon. She looked lovely in her perfect-fitting habit which seemed moulded on her figure; the exercise and the air deepened the faint rose of her cheeks, and the sun filtering through the trees assailed her with little golden arrows which became prisoners in her chestnut hair. People stared at me as I rode beside my aunt, and I felt that the question on everybody's lips was, "Who is the girl?" I was pleasantly conscious that I looked my best, and that my hair was quite pretty as it floated behind me in a long fair mane.

We cantered to the end of the Prater, and the Empress told me we were going to visit the group of cottages and stables owned by the gentlemen riders of Vienna. There were lots of men about, including some Hungarians, and my aunt introduced me to Count Nicholas Esterházy, a smart black-eyed man with whom she seemed to be on terms of great friendship. Then we rode back through the cheering Vienna crowds, and, leaving our horses at the cottage, drove toSchönbrunn. I had a delightful afternoon, and the only thing which detracted from my enjoyment was the tangled condition of my hair; but I reflected that the inconvenience was nothing and, *"Il faut souffrir pour être belle."*

The next evening we were invited to a family dinner, and there I saw, for the first time since I was quite a tiny child, my cousin the Crown Prince Rudolph.

When he entered the room I experienced a curious feeling of uneasiness. Perhaps my subconscious self knew the danger which Rudolph was destined to become in my life, and my nervousness increased when I saw that he watched me narrowly out of the corners of his eyes. The Crown Prince sat next to me and commenced to tease me unmercifully, and, boy though he then was in years, he seemed to possess the intelligence of a man. He was handsome, and for some time I racked my brains to remember what wild animal he recalled to me, for he had a curious look not altogether human. Then, I knew - Rudolph reminded me of a wolf; his eyes blazed green at times, and he seemed almost ready to spring. "Was he as cruel as a wolf?" I wondered, and then an icy chill went down my spine as I recalled the Empress's words to me before dinner when I had gone to show her my pretty gown. "Marie," she had said, "to-night you will see Rudolph. I warn you against him, because he will turn on you if ever he gets the chance."

I glanced apprehensively at my cousin, who was mimicking his father's habit of twisting his moustache, for Francis-Joseph couldn't sit for five minutes without making sure that his moustache was still on his face. The Emperor was very kind to me, and told me as a huge joke that I was not a child, but just a Bavarian broomstick.

After dinner I went with my parents to the Opera, but before we left, my aunt told me to come to her boudoir. Here she gave me a beautiful diamond hairpin, and fixed it in my hair, which she had stipulated must be dressed in heavy plaits like her own. We sat in the Emperor's private box, and I remember that many people stared at me; but, happy in my white lace gown and glittering diamonds, I felt I could brave criticism, and so I did not mind very much the curious glances which were directed at me.

In the middle of the performance I felt very hungry, for the family dinner was by no means a banquet; so, during the *ent'racte* I whispered to papa that I should like something to eat. But I was not prepared for the wrath which followed this simple request. "Another word and I will box your ears," he hissed. "How dare you be hungry at the Opera! And if you are, listen to the music and feed on its beauty." I tried to follow his advice, but I felt really sinking, and although I adored the Opera, I was very glad to get back to Schönbrunn and supper.

Our delightful stay in Vienna came to an end all too soon, and we returned to Munich. After I had been a few days at home, I received the following telegram: "I give you Mary, the little mare you rode at Vienna. She arrives by the next train, and she is your very own. Aunt Elizabeth." I went nearly mad with joy at this fresh proof of my aunt's affection, and I called to mind her parting words to me: "Go on as you are doing, and you will see me again." I felt sure that the Empress trusted me, because on several occasions I had been asked strange questions, to all of which I had answered, "I don't know." Something told me that she herself had put me to the test, and that "I don't know" was exactly what she wished me to say.

When I was sixteen years of age, I had several proposals of marriage, and my most ardent suitor was Count Herbert Bismarck, whom I knew through my great friends, the Princesses Wittgenstein. Laura, the eldest, was much older than I, and she was a lovely woman, who was greatly admired by the late King Edward VII. Herbert Bismarck proposed to me through "Lizzie" Wittgenstein, but as I did not take his proposal seriously, Lizzie interviewed mamma, who promptly went to ask advice from my grandmother, the Duchess of Bavaria. Grandmamma, however, declined to discuss my matrimonial affairs, and told my mother that she had better speak to King Ludwig on the subject.

The King, who liked me, strongly objected to the proposed match, and said with great decision that he would rather see me dead than married to a Protestant.

After that, mamma declined the honour of a Bismarck alliance, and I did not see my disappointed lover until next May when we went to Kissingen where my aunt the Queen of Naples was staying. Herbert, who had arrived to join his father at Kissingen, was apparently still very much in love with me. One day I received a passionate love letter from him in which he begged me to elope and defy King Ludwig, going on to say that he would wait for me outside the hotel on the following evening.

"He takes too much for granted," thought I, but I was curious enough to see whether he really meant what he had written, so, from my window on the third floor, I watched Herbert walking to and fro, until, convinced that it was hopeless to expect me, he disappeared in the darkness, and temporarily passed out of my life. It was not until years afterwards in Vienna that I saw him again - when I was Countess Larisch.

At Kissingen I received an unexpected letter from the Empress Elizabeth, who was going to stay at Feldafing close to Possenhofen. She told me I was to join her at once and to bring my horses. "We shall be quite alone," she wrote, "for I intend to dispense with a lady-in-waiting."

Needless to say, I went to Feldafing as soon as I could, and every minute which separated me from my idolized aunt seemed an hour. I made no pretence of hiding my adoration for her, and in spite of her habitually cynical manner, I think she was secretly touched and flattered by it. After all, what is purer and sweeter than a young girl's affection? The morning of life is always the best, and a love which has not sinned or suffered has an appealing purity all its own.

At this time I did not quite understand the Empress. I loved her, and she fascinated me, and gradually, as she took me into her confidence, she told me how irksome she found her life, and how much she hated the pomp and circumstance which surrounded her as Empress of Austria. "I hate the ceremonies of life," she declared. One thing struck me forcibly at this real beginning of our intimacy, and that was my aunt's absorbing passion for her beauty. She loved her loveliness like a Pagan, and she worshipped it as well. The sight of her perfect body gave her pure æsthetic delight; anything that marred its perfection was inartistic and distasteful to her, and she told me with almost painful frankness how she loathed the periods of child-bearing which had temporarily disfigured the symmetry of her figure. "Ah, the horror of growing old," she exclaimed, "to feel the hand of Time laid upon one's body, to watch the, skin wrinkling, to awake and fear the morning light, and to know that one is no longer desirable! Life without beauty would be worthless to me."

The Empress and I walked together early every morning; she then bathed, her hair was dressed, and afterwards the whole family met at breakfast, which was exactly like a meal at a restaurant as everybody ordered something different. My

38

grandmother came over from Possenhofen; the Queen of Naples and Duke Karl Theodor and his wife and children were also present; from Munich came the Empress's eldest daughter, the Archduchess Gisela; but Rudolph was not one of the party, and I did not regret his absence.

After breakfast we took grandmamma back to Possenhofen; she was a very dignified old lady who never went anywhere without her two little white Spitz dogs, whose mission in life was to endeavour to bite everyone with whom they came in contact. We generally dined at Possenhofen, and then I rode alone with the Empress in the cool of the evening. Ah! how I remember those happy days. Together we rode through deep woods where the sound of our horses' hoofs was deadened on a fragrant carpet of pine needles; together we startled the furtive wild creatures, and together we watched the sunset, and saw the rising of the moon.

I looked upon Elizabeth as a being from the old world of the Gods. She was Artemis - cold, beautiful, and arrogant. I saw her in fancy passing through the forests with her hounds hot on the trail of the deer. Again I pictured her ivory loveliness gleaming in the moonlight when she bathed, like Venus - and in those scented solitudes she was like a Pagan called back from the Past.

One day when we had ridden far into the woods, we came upon a tiny lake covered with water-lilies. Overhead it was canopied by trees, and the still surface looked almost black, for no light penetrated through the interlaced branches. The air was cool with the dampness of ferns and rain-soaked leaves which covered the ground, and sent up their fragrance to the hidden sky. It was an eerie place, but it appealed to the Empress; so we dismounted, the groom took the horses, and we walked over the spongy turf to some flat moss-covered stones which were close to the water's edge.

"Let us sit down," said Elizabeth; "ah ... this place must be the haunt of nymphs and wood fairies." She gazed for a long time, without speaking, at the lily-covered water. Then she turned to me: "Do you like fairy stories?"

"Yes, very much, Aunt Cissi," I replied.

"I'll tell you one of which this lake reminds me. Listen.

"Once there was an unhappy young Queen who had married a King who ruled over two countries. They had one son, but they wanted another, to succeed to the other kingdom, which was a lovely land of mountains and forests where the people were romantic and high-spirited. No child came, and the young Queen used to wander alone in the woods and sit by just such another lake. One day she suddenly saw the still surface move, the lilies parted, and then a handsome man appeared, who swam towards her, and presently stood by her side.

"The young Queen was frightened, but the stranger told her not to be alarmed. 'I am the spirit of the lake,' he said, 'and day by day I have watched you weep by the water's edge. Your tears have turned to pearls, and they lie in a golden casket in my palace below. Come, forget the world, and you shall be my Queen and reign happily with me.'

"The young Queen looked at the Water Spirit and sighed. How different he seemed from the King her husband! He wore a shimmering coat of mail, fashioned from the wings of dragon-flies, his bearing was noble, and his handsome, expressive face was lit by large black eyes, in whose depths the Queen read his ardent love.

"'I cannot come with you,' she said, but as she spoke, a strange drowsiness seized her, and leaning her head on the spirit's shoulder, she slept; he lifted her in his arms, and at his bidding the lake opened, and the waters formed a crystal staircase, down which he carried her.

"When the young Queen awoke she found herself in the magic country at the bottom of the lake. The palace was gay with water-flowers, corals, and shimmering shells, and strange-coloured fish looked at her as they swam past the transparent walls. Her lover adorned her with her tears, which were now long ropes of pearls, and the young Queen was astonished to see how many she had shed, but she remembered that woman's tears are said to be as countless as the sands of Time.

"At intervals the sun flooded the dim light beneath the waters with amber, and sometimes his dying rays tinged it with blood. At night the moon pierced the hearts of the cold flowers, which only unclosed for love of her, and then the fairy kingdom shone with a blue radiance.

"Beautiful nymphs sang and danced before the captive Queen, and twined her heavy hair with gleaming aquamarines and those many-coloured stones which are found in the Rhine. She sat beside her lover on his crystal throne, and slept in his arms on a bed of lily leaves; but after a time her heart ached for the land above the lake, and she entreated him to let her return. At last he consented, so the water nymphs carried her to the surface, and laid her on the grass under the trees, where the sun and the strong wind kissed her back to life, and then she returned to the King's palace.

"Some months passed and the Queen knew that she would have a child, and she longed for a son like the Water Spirit, who would reign over the romantic country of mountains and forests which she loved.

"But no son came, for when the child was born, the young Queen pressed to her heart a little daughter, with her Fairy father's large black eyes."

"Did she ever see him again?" I asked much interested.

"I do not think so," replied the Empress; "when you have more experience of the world you will realise that a baby is the end of many love affairs."

"What did the King say?" I queried.

"He had too much vanity to say anything, whatever he may have suspected," said Elizabeth; she laughed her mocking laugh, and was her cynical self again. .. We rode home in silence.

Life was very pleasant at Feldafing, and I was always glad to see Duke Karl Theodor and his second wife Marie-Josepha, who was an enchanting creature, brimming over with high spirits and twelve years younger than her husband.

She used to laugh at Princess Gisela, who copied everything she wore, and one morning Marie-Josepha appeared wearing a little straw basket upside down on her head. This, she told Gisela, was the latest Parisian fashion in hats for the day after to-morrow, and when Gisela hastily invented a pretext to return home, Marie-Josepha was highly amused, for she knew that Gisela's sudden journey was solely to command her Munich modiste to procure her a similar straw hat at any price.

Marie-Josepha, who was an Infanta of Portugal, was very kind to me and I remember her with much affection. She always assisted her husband in his operations as an eye specialist, and took the greatest interest in his two hospitals at Munich and Tegernsee.

The Emperor occasionally came to Feldafing for a few days, but he did not like the place. Francis-Joseph did not care about wearing mufti, and the Empress used to annoy him by saying that out of uniform he looked for all the world like a shoemaker in his Sunday clothes. Elizabeth never called Francis-Joseph by his name, but invariably addressed him as "Du" (thou). "'Du,' come here," she would say to the autocrat of Austria, before whose power the whole of his family trembled, and at whose command defiant archdukes went into exile.

But "Du" could sometimes hold his own with his wife. The Empress always spoke in a very low voice, and kept her lips close together; this, and a curious habit of dabbing her mouth constantly with her handkerchief, were due to the fact that her teeth were bad, and she hated showing them. Unless one knew Elizabeth very well, it was difficult to catch what she was saying, and as no one dared ask her to repeat her words, conversation between the Empress and strangers was often a case of cross questions and crooked answers.

I imitated most of my aunt's peculiarities, and so I pursed up my lips and spoke in subdued tones when the Emperor on a particular occasion addressed me.

"For Heaven's sake, Marie," shouted the exasperated "Du," "open your mouth when you talk to me - I'm sure it's large enough - and don't get affected, like your Aunt Cissi," whereupon Elizabeth made a perfectly inaudible remark.

Two hours' ride from Feldafing, on the opposite side of Lake Starnberg, was one of King Ludwig's castles, and the Empress, who was very fond of her cousin, often used to go and see him there. One day she asked me to accompany her, and as I had not seen the King for a long time, I was glad of this opportunity of renewing my acquaintance with him.

The Empress went into the castle alone, and told me to wait in the Park, for Ludwig was even then a man of moods and had to be tactfully handled when an uninvited visitor was in question. After what seemed quite half-an-hour's wait, the King's valet appeared and conducted me to the castle. I dismounted, and ruefully surveyed myself in the many mirrors, for I was covered with dust and well-nigh choked with it, after our long, hot ride.

I was ushered into a darkened room, and could discern my aunt seated in an arm-chair close to where Ludwig was lying on a *chaise longue* with his head enveloped in cotton-wool and bandages. The royal sufferer was the victim of a bad toothache, which attacked him periodically, as a result of his over-indulgence in sugar.

A little table, covered with bottles of all sizes, stood at his elbow, and, as I approached, Ludwig feebly waved his hand, but said nothing. Elizabeth tapped my arm and whispered, "Don't laugh," then aloud she said, "The King would like you to sing; go into the music-room and sing Elsa's music from *Lohengrin*."

I was not overpleased, for my throat was gritty with dust, and I felt I could not do myself justice. "This will be a Swan Song with a vengeance," I thought, as I seated myself before the piano. I was horribly nervous, and as I had no music I sang and played many false notes. However, as Ludwig was obsessed by the toothache, and only required to be soothed somehow, and as my aunt was not at all musical, it did not signify much, so I attacked Elsa's score until the King took pity on me and told me I need not play any longer.

When I came back into the darkened room Aunt Cissi was saying good-bye to the King, who rose from his chair and kissed her hand. I could hardly refrain from laughing, for Ludwig looked indeed an object for mirth. He was the tallest man in Bavaria, and as the bandages which had been tied round his face were left with long upstanding ends, his head looked somewhat like a large white owl's. He graciously extended his hand for me to kiss, and as he did so I was nearly overcome by the mingled odours of laudanum, chloroform, cloves, camphor, and other toothache cures, which it exhaled.

Half-way to Feldafing we were overtaken by a storm, and in a few moments we were soaked to the skin by a down pour of tropical rain. We took shelter in a cottage which was used for storing hay, and which was occupied by an old woman who we heard afterwards was the widow of a fisherman. She did not recognise the Empress, who asked her if she lived there quite alone.

"Yes - quite alone," answered the woman, "but I am always waiting for my son to return."

"Where is your son ?" inquired Elizabeth.

"He has been lying in the lake for seven years."

My aunt and I exchanged glances, and I shivered at this uncanny statement, which seemed horrible to hear as the lightning flashed and the thunder rolled around the cottage.

"He will return, continued the woman - and as she spoke the wind and the rain beat mournfully against the window - "he *will* return."

"When will that be?" said the Empress.

"When God wills," sighed the mother. "But another will take his place, and he who will do so is not far from this cottage."

Elizabeth did not ask any further questions, but she always declared that the woman's utterances were prophetic of Ludwig's death, which, strangely enough, fulfilled part of the prediction. The Empress told me to give the old woman a thaler, but she did not appear to understand the value of money, so I slipped it into her pocket, and as the storm was nearly over we rode off. A beautiful rainbow spread its coloured arch over the lake. "Now we shall be lucky because we have seen the rainbow," observed my superstitious aunt.

Next day Ludwig sent the Empress a magnificent basket of flowers. There was a lovely bouquet of jasmine for me, and on the card which accompanied it were four words, "For the little singer."

"Do you know what Ludwig said about you?" enquired the Empress. "He told me that you reminded him almost painfully of your Aunt Sophie.* Ah ... he will never forget her."

The delightful visit to Feldafing came to an end, and when I parted from Aunt Cissi she told me that I pleased her in many ways, and that she wished me to come to Gödöllő in September for some months.

* Sophie, Duchesse d'Alençon, younger sister of Empress Elizabeth, to whom he had briefly been betrothed and who died in 1897, one of many victims when a charity bazaar caught fire in Paris.

CHAPTER III
THE GUARDIAN OF SECRETS

Gödöllő - The education of a confidante - Aunt Cissi's circus - A family failing – Cub-hunting - "At break of day" - I renew my acquaintance with Count Nicholas Esterházy - Elemér Batthyány - His oath - He wishes to marry me - What did my aunt mean? - Her appearance on horseback - A "sewn on" habit - A strange kind of soup - The Emperor does not jump the ditch - "Nicky's" proposal - "Do not consult the Empress" – I confide in my aunt - What she told me in my bedroom - Why was she so perturbed? - "Bay" Middleton - His friendship with the Empress - Fallen among thieves - "Good-bye" - An interrupted farewell - The Emperor comes - The value of tact - The Crown Prince Rudolph at Gödöllő - I still dislike him - He questions me - "A bad-minded boy" – I box the Crown Prince's ears - "Rudolph is a very dangerous enemy"

In September my parents and I left Munich for Gödöllő. We travelled by special train from Pesth, and I made the two hours' journey in the same compartment as my horses, which were very fidgety and only to be quieted when I was near them.

The Empress met us at the station, mounted on horseback, and I can recall how striking she looked on that lovely autumn afternoon. She was delighted to see me, and papa and mamma were much pleased and flattered by her evident partiality.

Gödöllő is a hunting box in Hungary which belongs to the Emperor of Austria. The house is a large, long, low building with dome-shaped towers; close to it are dense woods, but the immediate surroundings are a kind of sandy scrub. Elizabeth herself showed us our rooms, but she did not sup with us and I did not see her again until early the next morning when I received a message that I was to go to her apartments.

Aunt Cissi gave me an affectionate "Good-morning," and then told me to sit down. "Well, Marie," she began, "you see I have fulfilled my promise to ask you here; do you also remember I suggested when we parted at Feldafing that you might care to remain with me until Christmas?"

"As if I could possibly forget," I exclaimed. Elizabeth smiled. "I have come to the decision to see a great deal more of you. Your father is my favourite brother; I love and admire your mother, and I wish to do the utmost in my power for you. But, Marie, my service is not a light one; it requires much which the average girl is not capable of carrying out. You are one of my own blood, and this constitutes a powerful tie. My position as Empress of Austria need never raise a barrier between us. I shall always be Aunt Cissi to you, and you will always be the dear little Marie who saw me cry and who never told anyone."

She pressed my hand and continued: "But listen, my child. At Gödöllő there is one thing to remember every hour of the day: *You must not speak of anything which you hear or see, and your answers to questions must be 'Yes' and 'No' or 'I don't know.'*

"I intend to keep you completely out of Court intrigues, and I want you to be careful of my lady-in-waiting, Countess F-, who is somewhat of a spy.

"Until cub-hunting begins I wish you to have dinner and supper with Valérie. She loves you, and I'm sure you will not refuse to gratify the child's fancy.

"I hope, Marie, I have not alarmed you by what I have said," she added lightly; "there will be a great deal to amuse you here; and now come with me and I will show you something of Gödöllő."

Elizabeth took me to see her little private circus, which was an exact copy in miniature of a large one. I think a penchant for circuses must run in our family, for my grandfather, Duke Maximilien, had a circus at Munich, where he himself performed to the intense delight of his relations, and, for my own part, I must confess to a love for the sawdust. At Gödöllő there was a professional ring-master, and many well-trained circus horses, which went through all the tricks of the *haute école*. They were pretty creatures, and it was certainly a charming sight to see my aunt in her black velvet habit riding her little Arab round the ring, although it was rather an unusual pastime for an Empress.

The first day of cub-hunting at Gödöllő began at 5 A.M., but we were up long before that. I drove with my aunt half-way to the meet, where the horses were awaiting us, and then we had half-an-hour's ride to where the field was assembled. Count Nicholas Esterházy, who was master of the hounds, and lived at Megyar, near Gödöllő, paid his respects to the Empress directly she arrived, and favoured me with a prolonged stare.

"Well, Baroness," said he, "do you remember seeing me a few years ago?"

I instantly recalled the dark-eyed gentleman rider at Vienna, but as I disliked Count "Nicky's" rough manner, I said coldly, "Oh, yes, I always remember people who stare as rudely as you do." He laughed, and said something in an undertone to Elizabeth, who smiled, and we were soon surrounded by a crowd of gentlemen who were all anxious to be noticed by the Empress. Amongst them were Aristide Baltazzi and the charming Count Elemér Batthyány, the son of a celebrated victim of the Hungarian Revolution. His father, Count Louis Batthyány, was condemned to death by the Emperor, but he eluded the executioner by poisoning himself in prison, and the heartbroken widow made her son take an oath never under any circumstances to speak to Francis-Joseph.

The Empress was very fond of the Batthyánys; indeed, Elizabeth, who always coquetted with the Revolutionary Party, honoured Count Elemér with many proofs of her friendship.

The Count never forgot his oath, and although he often saw the Emperor in the field, he never acknowledged his presence in any way, and, strange to say, Francis-Joseph never resented this open rudeness; in fact, I think he rather admired the attitude of the Hungarian noble. He was the most handsome man I have ever seen, and his melancholy expression alone made him appear interesting and romantic. Count Elemér was very nice to me, and I saw a great deal of him; we often rode together, and gradually, during those pleasant days, our friendship became something akin to love. One morning, when we were riding under the autumn leaves, the Count asked me to marry him. I could not, of course, give him a definite answer, for my duty to the Empress only allowed me to say, "I don't know."

Elizabeth's shrewd insight enabled her to read my secret quickly, and on the way back to Gödöllő she asked me point-blank how I liked Count Elemér.

"He's certainly very charming," I faltered.

"Would you marry him?"

"Oh, Aunt Cissi, I can't answer that at once."

"Well," said Elizabeth lightly, "I'm inclined to think it might be a good match; you might influence him to be friendly with the Emperor. But, my dear Marie, Elemér as a husband would be very disappointing."

"Why?" I queried.

"Never mind why," she rejoined; "you would soon know *why* if you married him."

I confided my aunt's cryptic remarks to Count "Nicky" Esterházy, and asked him if there was anything dreadful in Elemér's past life. "Nicky" was extremely amused at my question, and observed:

"Well, Baroness, all I can say is that there is nothing dreadful about Batthyány's past. It is only his health which does not justify him in marrying." Then growing serious, he remarked:

"Your aunt is very selfish; she wants you all to herself, and even if I were to propose to you, she would no doubt warn you against me."

We hunted three times a week, and it was perfectly delightful. Elizabeth looked lovely on horseback. Her hair was plaited round her head, and she invariably wore a high hat; her habit fitted her tightly, and she was always sewn into it every time she rode. By this I mean that once the bodice was on, her tailor sewed the skirt to it, and I could never imagine the reason for this strange whim. The Empress wore high laced boots with tiny spurs; she put on three pairs of gloves, and her indispensable fan was always slipped in her saddle.

49

Elizabeth partook of a strange kind of soup before she went hunting. It consisted of a mixture of beef, chicken, roebuck, and partridge all boiled together, and it was stronger than the strongest beef tea. She drank two glasses of wine with her soup, and later when we drove to the meet, she had a light meal of sandwiches and wine.

My aunt was a perfectly fearless rider, and it was a never-to-be-forgotten sight to see her during a run. She loved horses, and, no matter how tired she was at the end of the day, she always went after changing to feed her favourites; in fact, I can truthfully say that we spent hours in the stables.

I used to ride with the Emperor when the Empress did not hunt. He was always very nice to me, and I think he was much better-tempered in those days than he is now, when only my cousin Valérie sees the really human side of him.

However, Francis-Joseph was very angry with me on one occasion. We came to a very broad ditch, and as I naturally expected him to take the jump, I did not stop when I was over myself to see whether he had followed me. Suddenly I discovered that I was alone, and when we met, later, the Emperor told me he was greatly displeased.

"But why?" I asked; "I never imagined the ditch was too broad for *you*, Majestät," but the frown on the Imperial brow told me I had only made matters worse.

I always think that Francis-Joseph's greatest asset in the way of popularity is his good-natured expression. His face is his fortune in this respect, for even in the late evening of his days he is invariably referred to as "that dear old man" or "that kind-looking old man," and, after all, these charming epithets should not be omitted from the record of the many virtues by which posterity will remember him.

One day "Nicky" Esterházy came up to me and, without any preliminaries, startled me by saying in his brusque way:

"It is a pity for you, Baroness, that you are being brought out here. But even now if you accept the right man, he will save you from the bad influences by which you are surrounded."

"Well, Count," I answered, "where is the right man?"

"He is here," said Esterházy gravely.

"Listen, Marie, I care for you, I would make you a good husband, and you will be far happier as my wife than as the confidante of the Empress. Think over my proposal," he continued, "let your own inclinations guide you, but I beseech you, Marie, do not consult the Empress first." That evening, true to my promise to repeat everything to Elizabeth, I told her about Count Nicky's sudden declaration. "What shall I say, Aunt Cissi?" I entreated. "Oh, ... say what you like," she answered, and I was not sorry when she bade me good-night, for she seemed in a very bad humour.

As I lay awake thinking what reply I should give Count Esterházy, my bedroom door opened, and to my utter astonishment the Empress, who carried a shaded lamp in her hand, entered the room.

Elizabeth was all in white; her hair was wrapped about her in a heavy mantle, and her eyes shone like a panther's, in fact she seemed so strange that I was quite frightened and waited, trembling, for her to speak.

"Are you awake, Marie?"

"Yes, Aunt Cissi."

"Well, sit up and listen to what I have to say."

I sat up obediently, and she continued in cold, decisive tones.

"It is my duty to tell you that Count Esterházy has a liaison with a married woman, who loves him. After hearing this will you accept his proposal?"

My outlook on life, which had considerably broadened since my arrival at Gödöllő, told me that endless nice girls would be doomed to spinsterhood if liaisons with married women were considered insuperable obstacles when a man wished to marry, but one glance at my aunt's face told me I dared not consider Count Nicholas in the light of a husband.

"I am waiting to hear your answer, Marie."

"Oh - I'll not marry him," I murmured; and then, regardless of Aunt Cissi, buried my head in the bedclothes and burst into tears.

When I next met the Count I told him very briefly that I could not be his wife.

"I might have been certain that you would tell the Empress before you gave me your answer," was his only comment on my refusal.

About this time Captain Middleton, the immortal "Bay" of hunting fame, came to Gödöllő on a visit to the Emperor and Empress. Elizabeth made no attempt to disguise her liking for the pleasant Englishman, whose acquaintance she had made in Ireland. Indeed we all thought he was a very charming person, for although "Bay" was not a bit handsome, he possessed a certain subtle attraction for women, and was excellent company; in fact no one was dull when Captain Middleton was present.

I remember a rather amusing incident connected with "Bay's" first visit to Pesth. He had expressed a wish to go there, and the Empress deputed one of the "custodians" of Gödöllő to accompany him and to bring him safely back. The consternation which prevailed when the custodian returned without his charge may be easily imagined. The Empress was distracted, but all the man could tell her was that Captain Middleton had gone off to explore for himself after having promised to meet him later at the Casino. We thought of murder or sudden death as "Bay's" fate, but after a sleepless night for some people at Gödöllő, a telegram eventually arrived explaining that the missing man was in the police station at Pesth. It appeared that after leaving his guide, the Captain had met a charming lady of indefinite social position who invited him to her house, and as "Bay" soon discovered that he had literally fallen among thieves, he thought it advisable to steer for the safe harbour of the police station, and, as he was absolutely penniless, he asked the superintendent to wire his whereabouts to Gödöllő.

Elizabeth was furious when she knew the reason of "Bay's" absence, but she soon forgave him, and we resumed our pleasant rides with the Captain in attendance. The Empress would often leave me with the groom and ride off alone with her English friend. Nicky Esterházy heard of this, and asked me whether it was true.

"Dear me, no," I replied, "I'm always there."

Nicky looked at me in a disapproving way, and remarked, "You are but a young thing, and it is ten thousand pities that you take to Court ways as a duck takes to water. My advice, little Baroness, is ... return to Munich before you are spoilt."

I tossed my head angrily. What right had Count Esterházy to reprove me? After all I was only obeying my aunt's instructions never to know anything when asked embarrassing questions. She was the best judge, and I would brook no outside criticism. I was still highly indignant when I repeated Nicky's words to the Empress.

Elizabeth laughed her little mocking laugh. "Oh, then, you're not so stupid as you look," she said, which was, to say the least, a compliment that might have been expressed differently.

I shall never forget the afternoon when Captain Middleton left Gödöllö. Elizabeth, who had cried at intervals all the morning, told me I was to sit in the room next to her boudoir when "Bay" came to make his adieux. The Empress's rooms had three doors: one opened into Madame Ferenzy's room, another into the room where I sat, and the third into a corridor.

I was getting tired of waiting when suddenly my aunt, who was wearing an exquisite tea gown, came in hastily and made a sign for silence. Her eyes were swollen with crying, and she said impatiently, "See who is at the door, Marie, for nobody must come in."

Then I heard some one knocking on the door which led into the corridor. I ran forward. "Who is there?" I asked. "The Emperor," replied a voice; can come in?" "Oh, Majestät," I stammered, "how unfortunate that Aunt Cissi is not able to see you. She is trying on some riding habits." "Oh, then, I'll return later," answered Francis-Joseph, and I heard the sound of his retreating footsteps in the corridor.

That evening my aunt seemed very depressed, but she told me I had displayed unusual tact in dealing with the Emperor. "You knew quite well that I should not like anyone to see I had been crying," she remarked.

I thoroughly enjoyed my long rides with the Empress, who sometimes took a fancy to dress as a boy, and naturally I had to follow her example, but I remember how ashamed I felt when I first realised how I looked in breeches. Elizabeth imagined that this mad whim was not generally known at Gödöllő, but it was much commented upon, although I believe Francis-Joseph never discovered what was everybody's secret.

The Crown Prince came to Gödöllő for the shooting; he was then about eighteen years of age, handsome, seemingly good-tempered, and very fascinating when he chose. But I had not lost my first feelings of dislike for him, and we frequently quarrelled. One day he began to tease me about Count Elemér. "You were brought here to marry a nice tame animal of mamma's choosing," he mocked, "silly little Marie, don't be so shy."

"So long as I'm not destined for you, it does not matter," I told him.

"Look here," said Rudolph, "you are always with my mother; tell me what she does, there's a dear."

"There is nothing to tell," I replied. But when I informed the Empress about her son's curiosity, she was very angry, and said: "He is a bad-minded boy, and you must be on your guard against him."

Sad as it is to relate, mother and son disliked each other. The Empress used to say that she was Rudolph's mother by accident, and all that has been written about her great affection for him is quite untrue. My aunt had no maternal love, except for Valérie; she thought her children added to her age, and she disliked anything which marked the flight of time, like a growing up family. "I want to be always young," she repeated over and over again to me.

Rudolph was very rude next day, for when he met me riding with Count Elemér, he pushed his horse between us, and laughed coarsely. I met him afterwards outside the stables, and at once demanded, "Why did you laugh at me to-day, Rudolph ?"

"Why did I laugh? Why, Marie, I'm always amused when I see love-sick girls. Elizabeth T- languishes over me just as you do with Elemér. The silly goose thinks I adore her, and so I can do anything I like with her."

"You are a bragging liar," I told him.

"Oh, am I ? Well, look here," and the Crown Prince opened his letter case and showed me a photograph of Elizabeth T- on the back of which she had written a passionate declaration.

"Give me that photograph," I said, "it's not right that a cad like you should possess it."

"My honourable-minded child, don't waste your breath on Elizabeth, for she is no better than most girls."

Thereupon I lost control of myself, and forgetting my cousin's rank, I boxed his ears.

Rudolph bowed meaningly. "I shan't forget this," he remarked.

At supper I told the Empress the whole story. "It was rather an indiscreet thing to do," she said, "for Rudolph is a very dangerous enemy."

CHAPTER IV
MARRIAGE WITHOUT LOVE

Those were very happy days at Gödöllõ. The Empress and I used sometimes to have supper with little Valérie, and the Emperor occasionally joined us. Thither, too, came "Uncle Nando," as Ferdinand, Grand Duke of Tuscany, was familiarly styled.

The Grand Duke always played the buffoon to amuse Francis-Joseph, and he succeeded uncommonly well. Elizabeth used to regard him with good-natured contempt, and I remember "Uncle Nando" as a kind, not over-tidy looking man, who was always trying to get up a flirtation with my mother. "Give me a kiss, Baroness," he said once in his jocular way, and mamma's serious answer made everybody laugh. "Well - I would," she replied, "but, honestly, you don't look clean enough to kiss!"

The Empress nicknamed the Grand Duke "the pearl fisher," because whenever a new baby arrived at Salzburg, Francis-Joseph bestowed a pearl necklace upon the little Archduke or Archduchess. "Here comes the pearl-fisher," Elizabeth would observe, as "Uncle Nando's" family increased yearly, "he will soon have a fine collection of pearls and children."

The Empress and I often supped alone, and when the meal was over my aunt would have the pins removed from her lovely hair, and allow it to fall over her shoulders.

She would talk freely when she was happy and gay and life seemed roseate, but occasionally she was morose and moody, and obsessed by the dread of advancing age. Her life's task was to keep young, and she was always thinking about the best methods by which she could preserve her beauty.

Elizabeth was not a believer in any special face treatment. Sometimes she only used a simple toilet cream; occasionally at night she wore a kind of mask "lined" inside with raw veal; and in the strawberry season she smeared her face and neck with the crushed fruit.

The Empress took warm baths of olive oil, which she believed helped to preserve the suppleness of her figure, but on one occasion the oil was nearly boiling and she narrowly escaped the horrible death associated with many Christian martyrs. She often slept with wet towels round her waist in order to keep its proportions slender, and drank a horrible decoction composed of the whites of five or six eggs mixed with salt for the same purpose.

Once a month Elizabeth's heavy chestnut tresses were washed with raw egg and brandy, and afterwards rinsed with some "disinfectant," as she termed it.

When the actual washing was over, the Empress put on a long waterproof silk wrapper and walked up and down until her hair was dry. The woman who acted as her coiffeuse was hardly ever seen without gloves, which she even wore during the night; her nails were cut close; rings were forbidden her; the sleeves of her white gown were quite short; and it may be almost truthfully asserted that the hairs of Aunt Cissi's head were all numbered.

The Empress affected little tight-fitting chemises, and her nether garments were silk tricot in summer and leather in winter. Her many-coloured satin and moiré corsets were made in Paris, and she only wore them for a few weeks.

They had no front fastenings, and Elizabeth was always laced into her corsets, a proceeding which sometimes took quite an hour. Her silk stockings came from the London firm of Swears and Wells, and in those pre-suspender days, the Empress attached them by ribbons to her corset.

My aunt's lingerie was beautiful and exceedingly fine in quality; her nightdresses were quite plain, but always threaded and tied with mauve satin ribbon. She never wore petticoats, and when she took her early walks in the summer, she slipped her unstockinged feet into her boots, and wore no underlinen of any description under her bodice and skirt. On these occasions Elizabeth disdained a hat, and her umbrellas, which were large, clumsy and leather-lined, were very inelegant and weighty to carry.

A passion for walking for four or five hours winter and summer alike was part of her daily life, and Elizabeth could even do nine or ten hours at a stretch without being fatigued. This was not the case, however, with her ladies-in-waiting, of whom it might almost be said that they walked themselves out of her service; and at last this excessive exercise played havoc with the Empress's constitution, as she only took sufficient food to sustain bare existence.

Elizabeth slept on a plain iron bedstead, which she took with her wherever she went. She scorned pillows and lay quite flat, probably because she had been told by some one that it was beneficial to her beauty.

The Empress hated perfume, and her *entourage* were forbidden to use it. She never cared for jewels, although she displayed splendid ornaments at Court ceremonies. Her fingers were always destitute of rings, but she wore certain ones on a chain round her neck. My aunt adored pearls, of which she possessed quantities of rare and beautiful specimens, and she frequently gave them the "sea treatment" which is supposed to preserve their purity and lustre.

Elizabeth spent hours with her tailor whenever it was necessary to fit her with her habits, for she was very difficult to please, and studied the cut and style mounted on the back of a wooden horse placed in front of a large mirror. "All is vanity," I can hear some people exclaim; but my aunt considered it her duty to dress the part of an empress. "The people expect me to look beautiful and elegant," she would frequently observe to me, "and I often think it a pity they cannot see sovereigns trapped out in the splendour of past days, like the kings and queens of romance. So many royalties are frumps, and they imagine that their rank gilds their clothes; but it is not so, and their subjects greatly resent their dowdy appearance. The Princess of Wales* is the only woman in Europe besides myself who makes dress a fine art, and part of her popularity is due to her knowledge of what is suitable to wear on all occasions."

One day I noticed a new face at the meet. My attention was attracted by a handsome woman who sat on her horse in a very huddled-up fashion. She was the Baroness Vetsera, mother of Mary Vetsera, whose name will always be remembered in connection with the tragedy of Mayerling. Aristide and Hector Baltazzi, the two brothers of the Baroness, were staying with "Nicky" Esterházy, and they all seemed to be on very friendly terms with the Emperor and Empress. Indeed, my aunt herself introduced the Baroness to me, a fact which completely refutes the statements that I did not know the Vetseras until long after my marriage.

Elizabeth told me a good deal of gossip about the Baroness, and then imparted the information that Rudolph was generally supposed to have found her extremely sympathetic when his thoughts first turned to love.

About this time the Empress decided to visit Prague, as she wished to hunt in Bohemia, and I accompanied her. We left Gödöllö about 8 P.M. in a luxurious special train, which consisted of a drawing-room car, next to which was the Empress's bedroom opening into mine. Her two maids and her lady-in-waiting

* Later Queen Alexandra of Great Britain.

59

occupied the next carriages, and there was plenty of accommodation elsewhere for the gentlemen of the party, who were to join the train two hours later.

I had supper with the Empress, who was in her gayest mood, and I remember she narrated a fable in which she figured as Titania, the Emperor as Oberon, and a young Hungarian officer, Count Imry Hunyadi, as a love-sick elf called Imo. The allegory referred to Elizabeth's early married life, when she went to Madeira after a severe illness. Count Hunyadi was one of her suite, and I do not know what actually happened, but I *do* know that the Chamberlain spied most effectually on my aunt. The Count was recalled to Vienna, and Elizabeth's stay in Madeira came to an abrupt conclusion.

I drank a good deal of Bavarian beer at supper, which made me very sleepy, so my aunt sent me off to bed. Her women then came and undressed her, and soon the only sound to be heard was the noise of the train as it rushed through the darkness.

When we reached Pardubitz next morning there was a great gathering of the Bohemian aristocracy, and a good many presentations were made which greatly bored my aunt, who was delighted when she and I were in the carriage on the way to the Imperial horse-breeding establishment of Kladrub.

I slept in the sacristy of the chapel, and the moonlight streamed in through two long unshuttered windows which looked on the gardens. I was up early in the morning and drove with the Empress to Pardubitz, where the gentlemen were staying, and where I was introduced to Prince and Princess Furstenberg. The Prince was. Master of the Hounds, and the Princess was at one time a confidante of Elizabeth, but a coldness had arisen between them, and they had not met for some years.

After the Empress had visited the stables, we went on to Prince Auersperg's, where I saw the collected family of Larisch for the first time. My future husband, Count George, was then a shy little lieutenant, whose somewhat plain countenance was disfigured by spots.

My aunt went to bed that evening at eight, and I retreated to the sacristy and slept well in my sanctified surroundings. I was up betimes, and called by the thousand voices of the morning, put on my habit, and went off for an early gallop. Near Pardubitz I encountered Nicky Esterházy, who was also enjoying a quiet ride, and I hailed him with a cheerful greeting.

He did not return my salutation, but remarked, crossly, "It is very indiscreet of you to ride alone, Baroness. I wonder at your behaving in such a manner when you are staying with the Empress."

"Thanks very much," I answered. "Now, Count, don't let your horse take cold." And with this remark I left him.

I told my aunt about Nicky, but she only laughed.

"Why does this bothering man come everywhere with us?" I asked.

"Oh, Marie, after all he *is* so nice," was Aunt Cissi's reply. This remark, "Er ist aber so nett," was typical of her, and she always applied it whenever she spoke of people whom she liked.

After déjeuner we went over to Prince Kinsky's castle at Slatinan, where a great many smart people had been invited to meet the Empress. We were ushered with much ceremony into a large salon, and I began to understand the social value set upon me as the favourite niece of the Empress of Austria. We were offered tea, which Elizabeth never drank at any time, and I saw that she wore the cold haughty look habitual to her when "in harness," as she called those formal gatherings. Occasionally, when I met her glance, she made a disdainful little *moue*, and the tea-drinking was rather a fiasco, for the Empress did not attempt to put the guests at their ease.

I sat beside George Larisch, and decided that never in all my life had I met such a hopelessly dull young man. After being nearly frozen by the glacial atmosphere around me, I was overjoyed to escape outside with Aunt Cissi and inspect Prince Kinsky's famous stables. We duly praised his horses and hounds, and then said good-bye.

As we were driving home, the Empress remarked:

"What do you think of George Larisch?"

"I think he ought to do something for those spots," I replied; "and what a discontented, unhappy person he appears to be!"

"George is the nephew of old Count Larisch," said the Empress, "and both his parents are dead. His mother was the beautiful Hélène Stirbey, and his father died in a madhouse. George was educated by his uncle, Johann Larisch, and I think the poor boy has always been kept in the background. He has two sisters - Yetta, who married her cousin Heinrich, and Mitzi, who is not 'out.' So there, Marie, is the family history."

My aunt paused, and said rather gravely: "My dear, the day will come when you will have to marry. I should be dreadfully jealous of any husband who came between us, and who prevented my seeing you whenever I wanted. Now, I am certain that harmless little Larisch would never interfere with his wife's doings; he would be just the sort of useful husband to whom I should like to see you married."

"Oh, Aunt Cissi - I don't think I could ever live with a dull man like Count George!" I cried.

"As for that," answered Elizabeth, "a woman of our world has no use except for a dull husband; let the brilliancy come from outside. But, my child, think well over my suggestion, and if you could enter into this marriage, it can easily be arranged next season."

On the following day we went to Prague, as Elizabeth wished to visit the old Empress Maria Anna at the palace of the Hádràjin. As we drove through the town, the Empress told me that I must behave very discreetly, because I was going to meet the noble ladies of the Order of St. Theresa, who lived in retirement at the Hádràjin.

The object of this Order is to furnish a home for single ladies of illustrious birth, who receive an allowance. They are given suites of apartments in the palace, together with board from the imperial kitchens, and horses and carriages from the stables.

It is always presided over by an Archduchess, who, as Lady Abbess, has the extraordinary prerogative of crowning the queens of Bohemia; and when the. Cardinal Archbishop of Prague places the crown of Saint Wenceslaus upon the head of the Austrian Emperor when he is enthroned as King of Bohemia, it is the Lady Abbess of this Order who places the crown of Queen of Bohemia upon the head of his consort. It is the only instance where a woman is admitted to full episcopal functions by the Roman Catholic Church, and it is a privilege which has belonged to the Order for many centuries.

When we alighted from the carriage, Elizabeth whispered to me that I was to precede her, and as I entered the long vestibule I found myself in the midst of curtseying old ladies, one of whom rushed at me with a bouquet and kissed my hand. The Empress laughed immoderately, but the noble ladies failed to see the joke, and treated me to such hostile glances that I was glad to find myself safely in our apartments.

Aunt Cissi at once went to see the Empress Maria Anna, and I had supper alone in a large dark room. I had just finished when the door opened, and Elizabeth entered accompanied by a very thin tall woman. My aunt made a sign for me to come forward, and I was then kissed by the stranger, who was none other than the Empress Maria. I remember that she made some kind remark, and then Elizabeth bade me good-night, saying as she did so, "Now, Marie, don't dream of old ladies, they're so unlucky."

I did not dream of old ladies, but next morning we had the bad luck to receive a telegram from Pardubitz which informed my aunt that a hard frost had set in. This put an end to all prospect of hunting, so we returned to Pesth, where we made our adieux to the disappointed gentlemen, and the special train bore us swiftly back to Gödöllő.

I spent Christmas with the Empress and thoroughly enjoyed myself. There were many festivities, and the peaceful, happy, intimate feeling of the season was everywhere. Three large Christmas trees were laden with presents, and Rudolph and I shared a table between us which was covered with bonbons. I remember so well how he teased me by nibbling off the ends of my sweets, and then replacing them in the satin boxes.

The Emperor gave me a beautiful black enamel cross set with diamonds, some handsome bracelets, and dainty fans. Aunt Cissi gave me lovely gowns that could only have been created by a great Vienna dressmaker, and last, but not least, I received a large album with a painting of Gödöllő on the outside, and filled inside with photographs of the most prominent members of the hunt.

After Christmas I returned to Munich. My governess and my father's adjutant brought me home, and we broke the journey at Vienna in order to remain a night at the Hofburg.

Much water had flowed under the bridges since I had left home. I felt I had somehow undergone a subtle change, and that I could never be quite the boyish, open-hearted Marie von Wallersee again. The Empress completely dominated my imagination; I knew I was not altogether improved by her influence, but I could not resist her charm, and when I realised that I was miles away from Aunt Cissi my heart ached for her, and I longed to see her again.

I went to my first ball in the early part of the year, and my beautiful white lace gown, trimmed with bunches of roses, was a gift from the Empress. The sight even of her handwriting made me miserable, and I detested the nice ordinary people with whom I came in contact. Then something seemed to tell me that perhaps Elizabeth intended me to feel her loss, and that she wished me to find my own remedy. I suddenly remembered her words as we drove from Prince Kinsky's. Perhaps George Larisch as a husband represented the way out of my troubles. Once married to him I should not be under anyone's control. I could go to Aunt Cissi whenever she wished, and my rapidly ripening knowledge of the world told me that I might perhaps be more useful to my aunt as Countess Larisch than as her little unmarried niece.

That year I met the Empress at Feldafing, but this time she had brought Countess Festetics with her, and the reason was soon apparent, as the Countess was very friendly with the Larisch family. Aunt Cissi spoke of my marriage, and I was so overjoyed to see her again that I would have accepted the devil himself in order to please her.

"I want you to go to Solza with the Countess and spend a week with the Larisches," she told me; "then you can both join me at Gödöllō."

Countess Festetics and I spent two days at Vienna before we went to Solza, where I was rapturously received and had a very happy time. I quite appraised my own value in everyone's eyes, and also I did not fail to see that the whole family looked upon

George's marriage with me as a certain step towards raising the Larisches to princely rank.

I saw a good deal of George, who was staying with his uncle, and still thought him dull and uninteresting. "But," I reflected, "what woman ever marries the ideal man? Ideals are usually very troublesome to live with. As for love, it is not altogether desirable in marriage, for where love exists jealousy follows, and that invariably causes trouble. It is really far better to like and not to love, and I certainly can't say that I dislike George. After all he is one of the ordinary pleasant people who seem to be cast in the same mould."

Count Heinrich Larisch alone had the kindness to be honest with me. "I know it is the Empress's wish that you and my cousin should marry," he said, "but I feel it my duty to tell you that I am convinced such a marriage will not make for happiness. George is queer, his temper is uncertain, and he is obstinate."

"Aunt Cissi wishes it," I told him stubbornly, "and her wish is my wish." Therefore when George proposed to me that very day, I accepted him, but as he kissed me I felt like a dead creature, and I cried a little as I recalled my heroine's words, "My service is not a light one," for I was already beginning to feel the yoke.

I returned to Gödöllö as the fiancée of Count George Larisch, and the unfeigned delight which my aunt displayed made me more reconciled to my fate. The Empress wished the wedding to take place in six weeks, and I lived in a whirl of not unpleasurable excitement, for what young girl can resist the fascination of choosing unlimited new clothes?

Papa and mamma came to Gödöllö, but they took no active part in the preparations for my wedding. Aunt Cissi saw to everything. From Vienna came a positively imperial trousseau; Francis-Joseph gave me magnificent lace for my bridal gown, and the Empress presented me with a beautiful pearl necklace. I had quantities of expensive presents, and everybody, with one exception, congratulated me.

The exception was Count Nicholas Esterházy, whom I happened to encounter one day when alone. He looked at me with the greatest contempt, and said with brutal candour:

"Baroness, I cannot wish you happiness. I have no respect for a girl who sells herself to a monkey."

These were the last words which Nicholas Esterházy ever addressed to me, for wherever and whenever we afterwards met, he never took the slightest notice of me.

The Empress gave a soirée for me in the evening before my wedding, and just as I was coming down the staircase, I met the Crown Prince Rudolph, who was going up. He topped and informed me that I was the very person he wanted to see. "I have something to give you - here it is," and, as he spoke, he handed me a flat morocco case. "Open it," he added, "and tell me whether my little souvenir meets with your approval."

I opened the case, which contained a brooch set with an enormous black pearl. I started in dismay, for I have always had a dread of wearing black pearls.

"What! are you as superstitious as mamma?" asked my cousin. "My dear Marie, you are making your own misfortune in life by this foolish marriage; do you not honestly think it is a very mad scheme? Surely it is only to please mamma?"

Rudolph seemed so serious that I could not resent his plain speaking.

"It's too late now to reconsider matters," I told him.

"Well, don't blame my black pearl," was his retort.

The wedding guests assembled at the soirée; among them were Count and Countess Julius Andrássy with their daughter, Eleonor, Prince Kinsky and Prince Auersperg, who were George's groomsmen, and my bridesmaids, Finchi and Mitzi Larisch.

Uncle Nando was naturally included in the party. He loved family festivals because they represented plenty of good things to eat, and also because they gave him many opportunities of inflicting his well-worn jokes upon unsuspicious guests. I was glad however to see his cheerful face because I felt vaguely uneasy, and after all he was quite good-natured and far more of a human being than many of the others present. Dear little Valérie overwhelmed me with affection, and Aunt Cissi was more loving. than I imagined she could be; but somehow I wished I could awake and find everything a dream.

But my wedding day dawned, and I knew that I was face to face with the realities of life. It was October 20, 1877, and one of those days which are redolent of autumn. It was not my lot to be married in the season when the world is happy in the promise of spring, I was not to be a summer bride, walking on a carpet of roses, and feeling the splendour of love and noonday around her. I was married in the month which sets the seal of decay upon the last crimson and yellow leaves, and hurls them to the ground.

No summer sun shone for me; it was the season of departed hopes, and the few remaining flowers had shrunk shrivelled and dead before the early frosts which herald the coming of winter.

Almost mechanically I allowed myself to be dressed in my bridal robe of white silk covered with orange blossoms, which were arranged coronet-wise on my hair. My lace veil was fastened with diamond pins, and outwardly I seemed a happy young bride.

The ceremony was performed by a Hungarian bishop in the private Chapel at Gödöllõ, and afterwards a very elaborate dinner was served, to which Uncle Nando did ample justice. My gown was so tight that I dared not eat, and I was very glad to discard it for a more comfortable travelling dress. At last the hour arrived for our departure to Vienna; the Emperor kissed me kindly and wished me all happiness. Mamma and papa bade me the orthodox family farewell; Uncle Nando made a jocular little speech, and then Aunt Cissi, pale but lovely, came forward and took me in her arms. We clung together without speaking, regardless of those present.

The Empress cried bitterly. Perhaps at the moment of farewell, she felt some pity for me when she realised how blindly I had obeyed her wish that I should marry George Larisch. I cannot tell, but I always like to believe that such was the case.

CHAPTER V
A ROYAL INVASION OF ENGLAND

A honeymoon in Paris - London - We stay at Claridge's - Then and now - Mutual recriminations - The Empress arrives in England - Her advice - We go to Windsor – The late Queen Victoria - Aunt Cissi's comment - A reception at Count Deym's - Lord Beaconsfield - The Prince of Wales - A dinner party at Claridge's - The Prince of Wales suggests a whisky and soda - Combermere Abbey - Bay Middleton again - Hunting - We follow Bay - "Two's company" - I am lost - Count Larisch speaks his mind - How the best laid schemes "gang aft agley" - I am forbidden to remain with the Empress - We vegetate at Pardubitz - Baden-Baden - Louise, Duchess of Devonshire - I renew my acquaintance with the Prince of Wales - A fancy dress ball - Too many cooks - Louise receives a snub - Monaco - King Albert and Queen Carola of Saxony - Vienna - Elizabeth at the Hofburg - Her apartments - Fencing lessons - Aunt Cissi's supper parties - I meet Herbert Bismarck again - The Empress's superstitions - Her strange moods - The real Elizabeth - A Roman Empress - On the face of the waters - The woman who was - My aunt's faith in her convictions - Her opinions on love - Her contempt for life – Her unforgiving disposition

I spent my honeymoon in Paris, and like many another wedding trip it was not a happy experience, but my common-sense enabled me to see that I had no right to expect anything else. I had married Count George Larisch merely because it suited Aunt Cissi, and my chief attraction to him was my near relationship to the Empress of Austria.

I was quite prepared not to be happy, but I was not prepared to be made uncomfortable, and in those early days George displayed many of the peculiarities against which I had been warned by his cousin Heinrich.

From Paris we went to London to await the Empress, for Elizabeth had arranged to rent Combermere Abbey, and intended to hunt from there.

We stayed at Claridge's, which was then a dark uncomfortable place, and not, what it is now, a hotel where the spotless, beautiful rooms are a delight to see. When we arrived we found the King and Queen of Naples there, and I was delighted to see Aunt Sophia, for she had always shown me great kindness and affection. I think that she was really more beautiful than her sister Elizabeth, whom she copied in every possible way, and her most striking characteristic was her extraordinary good nature. The Queen was devoted to my father, and very fond of my mother, and as she was a level-headed, cheerful woman, I was very glad to be with her in London.

I had one or two distressing scenes with my husband after our arrival. I never seemed to please him. At first I cried, and then I lost my temper. "How stupid of *me* not to listen to Heinrich when he advised me not to marry you," I flared out one day. "How stupid of *me* to lower our family's prestige by marrying the daughter of an actress!" he replied.

This allusion to my darling mother stung me to the quick, and I retorted in no measured terms.

"My uncle is entirely to blame," bemoaned George; "his one ambition was to become related to the Imperial house, and my own inclinations were immaterial to him."

My husband was haunted by the fear of developing signs of his father's madness, and in his gentler mood he would beg me never to desert him if he ever showed symptoms of insanity, and above all, never to consign him to a *Maison de Santé*. I could not understand this fear, perhaps because I had become a fatalist in madness through seeing how unexpectedly it attacked the Habsburgs, and my own near relations of the Bavarian Royal House.

Count George and I met the Empress at the station, and she kissed me over and over again; then she returned with us to Claridge's, where a large suite of rooms had been reserved for her, and after she had talked for some time with the Queen of Naples, I received a message to go to her.

69

When I made my appearance Elizabeth surveyed me with a somewhat cynical glance. Then she said without preamble:

"Well ... how do you get on with George?"

"How do I get on?" At that my pent-up feelings gave way, and I told her everything. The Empress listened attentively, and remarked,

"What a pity he is so *difficile*! Anyhow, my dear child, you must make the best of a bad bargain; live without quarrels, and ... amuse yourself as well as you can." She shrugged her shoulders as she spoke, and I could see that George was dismissed as being unworthy of any consideration.

Elizabeth had brought her *entourage* with her, and I met my former acquaintances, Countess Furstenberg, Countess Festetics, and Dr. Wiederhofer. The Empress paid and received many private visits, and when I saw the beautiful Princess of Wales for the first time I fully shared my aunt's appreciation of her. The late Duchess of Teck, a handsome woman of opulent presence, brought her children to see Elizabeth, and I remember the present Queen of England as a pretty little girl, and thought her brothers very handsome boys.

One day the Empress told me she wished me to go with her to Windsor Castle. Aunt Cissi, who always admired Queen Victoria as a sovereign, deplored the dullness of her Court and the somewhat blatant domesticity which surrounded the throne, so I think she was secretly glad that our journey to Windsor only represented an afternoon call.

A Royal carriage awaited us at the station, and we drove to the Castle, where I sat alone for quite a long time in a very ornate apartment, until at last the doors opened and the Queen and the Empress came out together.

I remember thinking what a contrast the two ladies presented. Elizabeth wore a dark blue velvet gown trimmed with fur, a creation from the Rue de la Paix, and her hat was an exquisite affair laden with softly gleaming iridescent feathers. Queen Victoria was short and somewhat thickset, and she wore a voluminous black silk dress, partly hidden by an aggressive Indian shawl. An enormous white widow's cap surmounted her head, but nothing could detract from her pleasant homely countenance.

As the Queen entered the room I rose and made a deep curtsey. Aunt Cissi turned to her. "This is my niece, Countess George Larisch," she said, whereupon Queen Victoria extended her hand for me to kiss, and said a few charming commonplaces. Then we made our adieux and Elizabeth's only comment on the interview, was one long," Ah. ... I'm glad it's over!"

A few days after our visit to Windsor, Rudolph arrived, and one evening we went with him to a reception given by Count Deym, of the Austrian Embassy, who was related to my husband. At supper I sat next to Lord Beaconsfield, who talked mainly about his books, and was very anxious to know how they appealed to me. He struck me as being an exceedingly clever, pleasant man, who loved to live in the limelight. On my other side was Prince Radolin, and after supper the Prince of Wales (who had been watching Lord Beaconsfield and myself) said to Radolin, "That little Countess has made a conquest of Beaconsfield." "Oh, as to that," remarked Radolin, loud enough for me to hear, "the Countess will make many conquests." The Prince smiled and came over to where I stood. "Well, you have already charmed me," said his Royal Highness, and as he spoke he turned to Rudolph, and said laughingly, "I wish *I h*ad such a nice cousin."

George Larisch, who had overheard his harmless badinage, drew me aside regardless of the Prince's presence.

"For shame, Marie, you are behaving just like a Bavarian peasant," he said angrily.

"Oh dear ... what's worse than a jealous husband?" lamented Rudolph as he walked away with the Prince of Wales.

I was furious with George, and my pleasant evening was completely spoiled. Later on, Rudolph, who seemed in a devil-may-care mood, proposed that I should go back with him in a hansom to Claridge's, but my husband would not hear of this, so I had a dull drive with him instead.

One evening the Empress gave a dinner party, at which the Prince of Wales and the late Duke of Teck were present. I sat between them, and thought the Duke, who was in Highland costume, an exceedingly dull person, notwithstanding his handsome appearance. I was very tired, for I had been out in the country all day with Aunt Cissi, and the Prince, who noticed my fatigue, suggested that I should have a large glass of whisky and soda, which he declared would soon make me quite myself again. He was most charming, full of good-natured chaff, and I spent a very pleasant evening. After dinner there was a little ball. I danced two or three times with the Prince, and later on, when I bade Aunt Cissi good-night, I sang the praises of the Heir-Apparent. "Ah ..." said Elizabeth with a laugh, "I should think the Prince of Wales always gets his own way, so take care what you are doing, Marie." She did not, of course, make the latter remark seriously.

The next day we left Claridge's and went to Combermere Abbey, where Captain Middleton awaited our arrival, and Count Larisch and I took up our quarters in a hateful hotel at Whitchurch. Count Kinsky and his horses were already installed in the town, and every day we drove over in a dog-cart to see the Empress.

The hunting commenced soon afterwards. As we were unfamiliar with the rough country, the Empress and I always followed Captain Middleton's lead, and once, when Aunt Cissi gave up the run, I went on with Bay and secured the brush. We always dined at Combermere, and I remember how lovely Elizabeth used to look in the black or white velvet gowns which she invariably wore.

One day Aunt Cissi and I rode out alone with Captain Middleton. I was on one of Elizabeth's hunters, and when we had gone some distance the Empress told me to go back to Combermere. "I want to ride the mare to-morrow," she said; "so she must not get overtired."

"But, your Majesty," expostulated Bay, "the Countess can't possibly find her way alone."

"Well, direct her then," answered Elizabeth in a tone which admitted of no further argument; so the Captain then gave me such bewildering instructions as to which turnings to take that I naturally went in the wrong direction, and when it began to get dusk I realised that I was lost.

Darkness fell, so I inquired my way at a house, and as a kindly boy conducted me to the highroad I heard the sound of horse's hoofs and encountered Bay, who had come to look for me. He was quite out of breath and very much upset. "I think it was infernally stupid of 'Her' to send you away," were his first words, but I told him I was rather amused than otherwise, as being lost in England was quite a new experience for me.

When I reached home I found Count Larisch in the worst possible humour, so I did not dare to tell him about my aunt having sent me home alone. He was furious and would not listen to any explanation.

"There has to be an end of this Imperial slavery," he shouted. "I dislike the Empress, and I will not allow my wife to become involved in her intrigues. You must tell your aunt once and for all that I am not going to allow you to be at her beck and call. Your place is with me, and I intend to return home at once."

I was speechless with dismay when I realised that the Count really meant what he said. So this was the end of my hopes and of Elizabeth's plans for our uninterrupted intercourse! George Larisch, who had been chosen for my husband on account of his seemingly easy-going disposition, was not the man he had been estimated to be.

A wave of bitter anger swept over me. I had been sacrificed on the altar of a loveless union all to no purpose, and I felt like a prisoner for whom there is no escape.

I informed the Empress about my husband's outburst, but to my intense surprise she did not incite me to rebellion. "Say the word," I cried, "and I will leave George for ever."

"There must be no scandal," she answered; "perhaps, after all, it will be better to let him take you away."

"Oh, Aunt Cissi," I sobbed, all my fortitude forsaking me, "I only married because I wanted to be always with you."

"Man proposes, God disposes," was her laconic rejoinder, and I returned to the hotel in a very unhappy frame of mind.

We went back to Vienna a few days after my interview with the Empress, and she was apparently much affected when I took leave of her.

"Don't look so sad, dear child," she said, "we shall see each other again, and perhaps George will not be so offensive if he gets his own way in this matter."

George was, however, quite firm in his decision to keep me away from Elizabeth, and made me live chiefly at Pardubitz, where he had bought a castle. There I spent a quiet uneventful period, during which two of my children were born, and it was not until we went for a change to Baden-Baden that I had anything in the way of excitement.

The town was *en fête* for the Jubilee of the great races, and I met a great many people I knew there. My first visit was to the Duchess of Hamilton, a sister of the Grand Duke of Baden. I liked the Duchess very much, and I also saw her charming daughter Mary, who is now Countess Festetics-de-Tolna, but who was at that time married to the Prince of Monaco.

One Englishwoman was greatly in evidence at all the smart functions, but we were mutually antagonistic from the first moment of our acquaintance. This lady was Louise Duchess of Manchester, the "Double Duchess," as I have heard her described after she became Duchess of Devonshire. For some reason the Duchess did not like me, and as she had a very *mauvaise langue* she did not spare me whenever I happened to be the subject of conversation. The Prince of Wales was then at Baden, and as his Royal Highness seemed pleased to renew my acquaintance, the Duchess spread all kinds of scandal about our innocent friendship.

The Prince gave a very amusing fancy dress ball, to which the guests all came dressed as servants. He appeared as a chef, wearing the orthodox cap and apron, and presented all the ladies with charming souvenirs, mine being a gold chain bracelet, upon which was a ruby horseshoe. The Duchess watched me the whole time, and remarked, with the obvious intention that I should hear what she was saying, "Countess Larisch has evidently taken lessons in flirtation from her aunt, the Empress."

I repeated this to the Prince, who laughed, and told me to take no notice of the spiteful lady, who was further enraged when she saw his Royal Highness give me his arm and walk up and down the ballroom with me.

The Duchess also spread the story that I changed my hat three times during the long drive to the race-course in order to show that I disdained wearing any confection longer than a quarter of an hour. Louise, in addition, declared that I dyed my hair, and that a great deal of it was artificial. This amused me, so one evening I appeared at a ball with my thick fair hair simply arranged in two ribbon-tied plaits, which fell far below my waist, and the Duchess's statement was thus effectually disproved.

I spent two winters at Mentone, where we rented the Villa Michel, and one year, old King Albert of Saxony and his wife Queen Carola were stopping at the Hôtel d'Angleterre. They were very kind to me, and insisted upon my driving with them every afternoon, and I always attended Mass with them on Sunday. I used to call the King "Uncle" and the Queen "Tante" Carola. They were dear souls, who might have been mistaken for a simple professor and his wife when they walked out, for they did not look in the least like reigning royalties. There was some slight trouble regarding the relations between the Queen's lady-in-waiting and the Chamberlain, but Queen Carola prevented any scandal about the results by insisting that an immediate marriage should take place between the pair.

My husband and I had a flat in Vienna at 38 Praterstrasse, and our occasional residence in the capital had given rise to the absurd stories that I lived in a palace and gave great entertainments during the season. This is absolutely untrue; we rented the flat for two years only, and did not renew the lease. Afterwards whenever I came to Vienna I always stayed at a hotel. I went into society a great deal, and when the Empress was at the Hofburg, Count Larisch could not prevent me from being constantly with her.

The Hofburg is an enormous and most unhomely place, but my aunt's private apartments were lovely. They communicated by a corridor and staircase to a sort of annexe, occupied by her reader, which was quite separate from the Empress's rooms, and her ladies-in-waiting lived in another part of the Burg.

Aunt Cissi's drawing-room was all white; next to it was an uncomfortable dining-room, and then came the boudoir which was a study in scarlet. Her dressing-room contained an enormous toilette-table laden with crystal and silver, and a room beyond it was fitted up with all kinds of gymnastic appliances.

The Empress took her fencing lessons in this room, and she looked lovely in her short grey skirt and little coat of mail. She was instructed by the son of Herr Schültzer, my old master at Munich, and like everything else which she "took up" she fenced well.

This amusement replaced the circus craze, and Elizabeth, who then suffered from sciatica, did not hunt so much as formerly.

The Emperor's rooms were far away from Aunt Cissi's, and her doors were always guarded by soldiers. Francis-Joseph, who was very much in love with his wife, was often kept at a distance when Elizabeth's love of solitude obsessed her, and then she was never seen by anyone except the members of her immediate *entourage*.

The Empress gave delightful little late suppers when most of the virtuous inmates of the Hofburg were wrapped in slumber. I used to have some very happy evenings on those occasions, and it was at one of these suppers that I again met Count Herbert Bismarck, who was then an *attaché* at Vienna. Elizabeth was rather attracted by the Count, but somewhat resented his attentions to me until I explained to her that I had been the object of his youthful affection at Kissingen.

The Empress was very superstitious, and occasionally, when I had exhausted the gossip of Vienna, she would make me put the white of an egg into a glass of water, and together we would try to read omens in the shapes which it took. Elizabeth invariably made three bows to a magpie whenever she saw one, and the new moon afforded her the occasion to indulge in any longed-for wish. The Empress firmly believed in the virtues of cold iron, and she never passed nails or cast horseshoes without picking them up; the Evil Eye inspired her with real dread, and she feared the malign influence of those who possessed it.

Aunt Cissi once went incognita to consult a cardwoman, but she refused to disclose anything the seeress told her except a prophecy that she would never die in her bed.

"And that is most likely to happen," she said, "for when Valérie is grown up I shall travel in distant parts of the world, and one day I shall never return."

I was always interested in her conversation whenever she was the real Elizabeth to me - and I preferred her melancholy moods to her simulated gaiety. My aunt detested people who fawned upon her, and as I was never guilty of this fault we got on very well together. The sycophantic attitude of her family always irritated her, and she often quarrelled with her sisters. "I wish I had been born in the streets and had never known my family," she once declared. Sometimes she became a prey to an unnatural hatred for her children. "Children are the curse of a woman, for when they come, they drive away Beauty, which is the best gift of the gods," she once said to me. Again my aunt would often express her contempt for her exalted position. "What's the use of being an Empress in these days?" Elizabeth remarked bitterly. "She is only a dressed-up doll. Ah, how I should love to have reigned in Rome; the Empresses of bygone days knew the splendour of life and love; theirs was no grey existence like mine, which is encircled by a ring of etiquette; those women ruled men, and I envy even the worst of them."

Her amber eyes shone as she spoke, and I could see that her imagination had transported her far from the icy formalities of Imperial Austria, to the throbbing, passionate life of Imperial Rome.

"But the time will come for me to be free," she continued, as if musing. "Marie, sometimes I believe that I'm enchanted, and that after my death I shall turn into a seagull and live on the great spaces of the ocean, or shelter in the crevice of some frowning rock; then I, the fettered Elizabeth, shall be free at last, for my soul shall have known the way of escape. If ever I am destined to become old, nobody shall see my face. When once I have been kissed by Time I shall veil myself, and people will speak of me as 'The woman who was.'" This strange idea probably accounted for the Empress's dislike of being photographed, for she rarely sat for her portrait.

My aunt was extremely kind, and so long as people did not offend her she was very generous to them. But it was excessively difficult to probe her real feelings, and I always felt that she never said exactly what she thought. Elizabeth set great value upon the honesty of her convictions. "What *I* do not mind doing, nobody else need cavil at," she often said. "Love is no sin," she would remark. "God created love, and morality is entirely a question for oneself. So long as you do not hurt anyone else through love, no one ought to presume to judge you."

Elizabeth's chief characteristic was her intense pride and her contempt for the life she was forced to lead. When once her anger was kindled against those she loved she never forgave them. Explanations and regrets were alike useless; the Empress was absolutely relentless, and regarded the offender as dead, a fate which I myself was eventually destined to experience.

CHAPTER VI
INDISCRETIONS AND ECCENTRICITIES

*Vienna - A visit from the Empress - Rudolph in search of a wife -
Princess Matilda of Saxony - Plain and good - A Belgian bride - The
shadowy third - Rudolph's marriage - Opinions differ - An uncertain
future - The 'Trumpeltier' - Quarrels - The beginning of the end -
The story of the yellow domino - Cyclamen-Magic - 'Tout lasse, tout
casse, tout passe" - Predestined to suffer - The real and the ideal –
Princess Metternich – More about the Empress - Katrina Schratt -
The degenerate Habsburgs - The Archduke Ludwig Victor - The
Archduke Franz Ferdinand - His marriage with Sophie Chotek -
Otto the evil - His drunken feats - Naked and unashamed - His
horrible death – An earthly saint - The last home of the Habsburgs -
Shades of the dead*

I sometimes saw Rudolph at the Hofburg, but we never exchanged
many words, and as he was usually engrossed in his own pursuits,
I did not often meet him elsewhere. The Crown Prince had
travelled a good deal, and rapidly developed all the fascination,
cleverness, and degeneracy which unfortunately distinguish so
many of the male members of the house of Habsburg.

About this time the Empress commenced to write the story of
her life. The work was set up in the cellars of the Hofburg, and the
type was afterwards distributed. Two copies of this extraordinary
autobiography exist and are in safe hands, but the book cannot be
published for another forty-five years.

Shortly after my daughter Mary was born, Elizabeth paid an
unexpected visit to the Praterstrasse one evening at nine o'clock.
As she came in she encountered the baby's wet nurse, a fat
Bohemian, who was dressed in a short skirt and a night jacket.
The poor woman, who was suffering from a bad cold, had plugged

up her nostrils with wool in order to prevent the baby catching it, and, lantern in hand, was just about to depart for her own room. Elizabeth declared that she took the nurse for a ghost, and afterwards teased me by frequently asking whether I *always* had my babies fed by lantern light.

The real object of my aunt's visit was to tell me that Rudolph was soon to set forth in search of a wife, and we felt rather sorry for the princess who would be honoured by his choice. Elizabeth quite realised her son's uncertain temperament, and we both knew that it would require a woman with exceptional tact to retain his affection or even his tolerance.

His first visit was to Dresden, as Princess Matilda of Saxony was considered a safe kind of girl for my volatile cousin to marry. Matilda was rather good-looking in those days, but Rudolph's artistic eye observed the first signs of the *embonpoint* which has since developed in her, and he felt that he could not face the future with such a wife. He, therefore, proceeded to Spain, only to find that while the selected Infanta was a very nice girl, her face was certainly not her fortune, and he decided that her ugliness would be worse than Matilda's bulk as a lifelong bargain.

By this time Rudolph was sick of travelling about to inspect princesses in whom he found neither intellectual nor physical appeal. He had inherited his mother's love of the beautiful, and I think he was really anxious to marry some one whom he could like. But his many adventures with charming and lovely women had made his taste ultra-fastidious, and therefore it is not surprising that he rejected the various dull, unattractive young girls who were suggested to him as possible brides.

At last Rudolph's wanderings led him to Brussels, when, weary of a choice of many evils, he decided to take the least of them, as represented by the Princess Stéphanie of Belgium. His proposal for her hand was jumped at by grasping old King Leopold, and the Crown Prince accepted his fate most philosophically.

When the first photographs of the bride-elect arrived at Vienna, everybody was quite startled to see how excessively plain she looked. The virtuous who knew Rudolph's past career shook their heads sadly and reflected that this was not the right wife for the Crown Prince, and the numerous ladies who knew and loved him were overjoyed to think that, with such a bride, there was no possibility of his ever becoming a model husband.

I am afraid to recall the many scandals which attended my cousin's courtship. It was generally known that Rudolph had taken a lady with him to Brussels, and that she had been discovered by the Queen and her daughter when they paid him a surprise visit. It was said that the match was nearly broken off in consequence, but nothing else untoward occurred, and the wedding took place at the Hofburg on May 10, 1881.

The marriage of the Crown Prince of Austria was naturally a splendid affair. I occupied the position of "Palast Dame" at the time, and by virtue of it took precedence of all other ladies. I wore a charming yellow and silver gown, with a blue and silver *manteau de cour* three yards long, which was carried by a page, and the display of beautiful jewels worn by beautiful women was perfectly dazzling.

The Belgian Princess looked her worst in her bridal attire; her arms were red, and her dull yellow hair was most unbecomingly dressed. Stéphanie was very tall, and her figure in those days was most deplorable, but since then constant care and a clever corsetière have remedied the defect. She had no eyebrows or eyelashes, and her one beauty was her exquisite biscuit-china complexion.

I could quite imagine what Aunt Cissi thought of Stéphanie, for one look at her face was enough for me, and Rudolph's expression was that of a man who is leaving a glorious past for a very uncertain future.

After the ceremony we all went into the great reception salon of the Burg, and Rudolph and his wife addressed a few gracious words to each lady present. When they came to where I was standing, the Crown Prince looked at me with a mocking glance in which self-pity was strangely mingled, and, turning to Stéphanie, he said: "This is my cousin Marie."

The Crown Princess embraced me and told me how glad she was to meet me; then they went off, and I remember feeling genuinely sorry for Rudolph as I reviewed my own loveless marriage.

I did not see the Crown Prince and Stéphanie until September of the following year. I had gone to Schönbrunn to meet my parents, and after supper I walked with the Empress in the little private garden. It was dark, and as we paced to and fro Elizabeth talked to me of many things, including Rudolph's marriage, which was even then beginning to prove a failure. The night was very still, and from the garden we could see the lighted windows above us, and the flight of stone steps down which we had come. Suddenly a servant hurried in our direction, and announced that the Crown Prince and the Crown Princess had arrived. The next moment we saw two forms silhouetted against the light, and then a figure came down the steps. It was Stéphanie. Elizabeth watched her progress with interest. "I did not expect to see Rudolph and the nasty 'Trumpeltier,'" said Aunt Cissi to me, as she advanced over the grass to welcome her daughter-in-law, who had really improved very much in appearance since her wedding-day.

Stéphanie was always exceedingly nice to me and when I had occasion once to ask for an audience with her she told me to come and see her in future without formality. I always think it regrettable that she was so much influenced by her sister, Princess Louise of Coburg, who fostered her jealousy and told her all kinds of things about the Crown Prince, who gradually found her unbearable to live with. Stéphanie made constant scenes of jealousy and anger, which made Aunt Cissi remonstrate with her about the scandal such dissensions caused. The Empress as a bride had learnt to suffer and to be silent, and she naturally expected her daughter-in-law to follow her example. Rudolph adored his little child, the Archduchess Elizabeth, who was born two years after the marriage, but Stéphanie made even the child a source of contention, and so my cousin's domestic life went from bad to worse, and we who looked on wondered what the end would be.

Society in Vienna was very gay in my time and we never interfered or bothered about each other's doings. I used to love going to the masked balls, and I remember once meeting the Baroness Vetsera (Mary's mother) and the Archduke William at a masquerade at the Imperial Opera House. The Baroness was resplendent in an orange-coloured domino, and when she and the

Archduke were sitting out together on a little bench, the old man, who loved to retail all the latest gossip, unwittingly informed her that one of the Esterházys, to whom she was much attached, was going to marry Eugenie Croy.

On hearing this the Baroness promptly fainted, and as the bench was not provided with a back she disappeared into space, and only a conspicuous display of shoes and stockings in the air marked her whereabouts.

Everybody laughed; and the Archduke, who was full of remorse when he realised the effect of his garrulousness, set about with wonderful energy to pull the lady round in more ways than one.

The orange domino worn by the Baroness reminds me of an interesting incident when Aunt Cissi once went to a masked ball, accompanied by the Archduke Ludwig Victor. Elizabeth and Ludwig were dressed alike in yellow dominoes, and no one present suspected their identity; in fact they were taken for sisters. Amongst the masqueraders was a good-looking young "Hofrath," who attracted the attention of the Empress, and entering into the spirit of the evening she went up and spoke to him.

The masquerader took the unknown lady to be some footlight favourite, and as their conversation progressed he became quite interested, and suggested that she should sup with him that night at one of the smart restaurants.

"Very well," said Elizabeth, who was entirely enthralled by the adventure. "I will come on condition that you give me your word of honour to allow me to retain my mask."

"Certainly," assented the enamoured gentleman. The Empress then asked her "sister" to await her return at a certain place, and left the ballroom with her admirer.

True to his promise the "Hofrath," never attempted to force Elizabeth to disclose her identity, although he had really fallen in love with her when the time came to say good-bye. The Empress promised to meet him next day, but naturally she never kept the appointment. Her romantic tendencies and the remembrance of that delightful evening caused Elizabeth to send her admirer an affectionate letter every year, signed "The Yellow Domino," but the curiosity of the recipient was never gratified by finding out who the writer was. These letters were posted in different parts of Europe, and the last one was mailed by one of my cousins at Rio de Janeiro. Elizabeth told me this adventure as a fairy tale, called "Cyclamen-magic," in which a beautiful sleeping girl is reminded of her happy hours by the fragrant cyclamen flowers. "Do you remember the yellow domino?" asks one; while another recalls to her the drive in the darkness, and a third reminds her of her lover's adoration. The Empress then explained the hidden meaning of the "Cyclamen-magic," but she treated the adventure lightly.

Elizabeth was in love with love because it represented the colour of life to her. She regarded the excitement of being adored as a tribute which her beauty had a right to demand; but her fancies never lasted long, probably because she was too artistic ever to become sensual, and the lover who shattered her conception of him as an ideal was instantly dismissed. "Tout lasse, tout casse, tout passe," might have been Elizabeth's motto throughout a life which was so full of disappointments, and she was one of those women who are predestined to suffer through their affections. Her real place was with the Immortals; she should have been wooed upon the fragrant slopes of Parnassus, or yielded, like Leda or Semele, to an all-conquering Jove. The grossness of life repelled the Empress just as much as its beauty attracted her, and I believe she was far happier when her eccentricities developed and she communed with ghosts in a world of shadows, or talked with the spirit of Heine, who, she imagined, inspired her compositions. Her shyness was solely due to the morbid dread that she would be thought less beautiful as she passed down the vale of years; and only those who, like Elizabeth, value their beauty because it attracts love can understand what she felt. The ordinary mind will deem her a vain and shallow woman, and reflect that true happiness can be found in one's children's children, but such people have not the artistic temperament which the Empress possessed.

Elizabeth was not at all popular in Viennese society; she kept herself aloof from it, and only went to one or two regulation balls during the season. I remember seeing her on the last occasion when she appeared at the Festival of Corpus Christi, as she walked through the three Courts of the Burg, looking like a lovely Queen of Romance in her grey silk dress and violet velvet mantle.

Princess Pauline Metternich has always been the acknowledged leader of society in Vienna. She is very smart, exceedingly clever, and can be exceedingly unkind. I always liked her, and I used to perform in many of the theatricals of which she was so fond. Her entertainments were splendid; she is a born hostess, a typical example of the "grande dame," who is unfortunately fast disappearing.

The Princess once came very late to a ball given by the Archduke Ludwig Victor. The Emperor and Empress had been there some time, and the host remonstrated with Pauline about her tardy appearance. "It doesn't matter when I arrive," she retorted contemptuously. "I'm always in plenty of time to see and hear as much of the Empress as I care for."

Elizabeth noticed them conversing, and afterwards asked the Archduke what Princess Metternich had said. Ludwig Victor was reluctant to repeat the rude remark which Pauline had made, but the Empress insisted. "Ah, poor Princess, if only she knew how she amuses me," observed Elizabeth, "for I never look at her face without being reminded of certain mischievous animals in my monkey house at Schönbrunn."

I think my aunt at first liked the excitement of being Empress, for the blood of my grandfather, who loved horses, women, and wine, flowed in her veins, and at first she demanded all that life could give her. My father told me that when Elizabeth first entered Vienna she turned all men's heads with her beauty, and that her after troubles originated with the unkind treatment which she received from the Emperor's mother during the first years of her married life. She was never allowed to be natural. Repression brought out the inborn eccentricities of her family, and when she discovered her husband's entanglement with a Polish Countess her affection for Francis-Joseph received a blow from which it never recovered.

Elizabeth's children were taken from her by her mother-in-law on the excuse that she was not fitted to be entrusted with their care, and I think this made my aunt almost dislike Rudolph and Gisela, and lavish her love on Valérie, who was entirely under her own control. Poor woman! small wonder that she became cynical and soured, and I am only surprised that she was not more so as time went on, when she realised that most of her ideals were illusions.

During the lifetime of the Emperor's mother, Elizabeth was virtually alone, and when the tyrannical old woman was dead it was too late to change. Hungary always appealed to her imagination, and she was never the haughty, reserved Empress of Austria to the people of the country of which Francis-Joseph was King.

About the year 1885, when the desire to travel first seized Elizabeth, her kind heart reproached her when she thought that her husband would perhaps be lonely during her absence.

"Do you know of any trustworthy person who would entertain the Emperor without trying to influence him?" she asked me one day.

I mentioned several ladies who, I felt sure, would only be too delighted to console the Imperial grass-widower, but Aunt Cissi did not approve of them, and the matter dropped until she suddenly told me one day that she had discovered the right person in the actress Katrina Schratt, who was always considered to be more interesting off the stage of the Burg Theatre than on it. She was, and is, a charming, simpleminded woman and my aunt thought very highly of her. Elizabeth used often to visit Frau Schratt, and gave her many presents, amongst them being a little churn of which Katrina was inordinately proud. People rather disapproved of Elizabeth's attitude, but she was quite right in thinking well of the actress, who has since the death of my aunt proved herself to be a devoted friend to Francis-Joseph.

Frau Schratt has a beautiful villa, in the Glorietstrasse at Hietzing, which is a perfect storehouse of lovely things and includes many presents from the Emperor. She also has a little cottage at Ischl, and whenever Francis-Joseph is there, Katrina is always at the cottage, and the Emperor invariably takes tea with her. There is an amusing story about an evening visit which the Emperor once paid his friend. He had remained rather late, and with his usual consideration Francis-Joseph, who did not wish to disturb the sleeping household, made as little noise as possible as he walked down a passage which led to the garden entrance; but just as he reached it a door opened, and Frau Schratt's new cook came out in her nightgown, carrying a lighted candle. The sound of footsteps had alarmed her, and naturally when she saw the figure of a man, her first impulse was to scream.

Francis-Joseph came forward quickly. "Be quiet, you stupid woman; don't you know me? I'm the Emperor," he said in a low voice.

The incredulous cook was taken aback, for in her wildest flights of imagination she had never pictured herself meeting the Emperor of Austria wandering about late at night. Still doubtful, she turned the light of the candle full on the stranger's face, and as she did so she recognised the well-known features of Francis-Joseph.

The loyal woman instantly fell on her knees and began to sing the National Anthem at the top of her voice. The Emperor made a hurried exit, and I doubt whether a patriotic hymn has ever been sung under more ridiculous circumstances.

The Emperor has certainly been most unlucky in his family circle, for the shadow of madness dogs the footsteps of the Habsburgs, and there is hardly any branch of the family which does not possess some insane, epileptic, or vicious member. It is lamentable that the healthy children of Franz Ferdinand and Sophie Chotek are debarred from the succession, as the baby who in the ordinary course of events will one day become Emperor of Austria has the possibility of inheriting, from the maternal side, the imbecility which characterises many of the princes and princesses of Bourbon-Parma.

Hardly a year passes without the outside world becoming cognisant of the vagaries of the Archdukes. The Archduchesses are easier to handle, for their parents usually permit them to marry the men of their choice, warned to do so, perhaps, by the fate of Princess Louisa of Tuscany, whose marriage to King Frederick August of Saxony was the cause of many of her subsequent troubles.

The Archduke Ludwig Victor is the Emperor's youngest brother, and I remember him as a gay, gossip-loving man, whose entertainments were a great feature of smart Vienna life. There were various rumours that the Archduke was somewhat addicted to vices which were only tolerated in the days of ancient civilisations, and eventually the Emperor decided that the air of Salzburg would be beneficial to his brother, and intimated to him that he must take up his abode there. So the Archduke disappeared from society, and Vienna knows him no more.

Francis-Joseph's second brother, the late Archduke Karl Ludwig, had three sons by his marriage with Princess Annonciade of Bourbon-Sicilies, and the eldest is the Archduke Franz Ferdinand, who will succeed his uncle as Emperor of Austria.

Franz Ferdinand is best known to the public by his morganatic marriage with Countess Sophie Chotek, who was formerly lady-in-waiting to the Archduchess Isabella. The Countess and the Archduke had a secret love affair, and one day at Pressburg everything was discovered through a lost locket which contained a photograph of Franz Ferdinand. The Archduchess immediately dismissed Sophie Chotek, but her lover lost no time in making her his wife.*

The Emperor soon realised that the marriage was a complete success, so he created the charming lady Countess Hohenburg, and afterwards raised her to the rank of a Duchess.

The Archduke Karl Ludwig, who was a fat old man of brutish instincts, married the Infanta Marie Therese of Portugal as his third wife. She was a lovely woman, fifteen years younger than her husband, whose chief recreations were riding, shooting, and ill-treating her. When the Archduke died it was generally supposed that his widow would marry her chamberlain, Count Cavriani, and there was a tremendous fuss about it.

The name of the late Archduke Otto, who was a very handsome man, is generally execrated in Austria on account of his many and varied wickednesses. I always think that the early training of the Habsburgs encourages whatever vices are lying dormant in them; for self-indulgence, idleness, and dissipation generally develop their hereditary failings.

* The Archduke and his wife, later created Duchess of Hohenberg, were victims of the assassination at Sarajevo on 28 June 1914, thus precipitating the outbreak of the First World War.

Otto married Princess Marie Josepha, a sister of the King of Saxony, one of the best of women, whom he systematically neglected from their wedding day. One evening, the Archduke went with some women to supper at Sacher's, where he had luckily engaged a private room. Suddenly he appeared shockingly drunk on the staircase of the restaurant minus all clothing except his gloves, his cap, and his sword. The intense horror of a highly respectable Count who had brought his daughter to supper is better left to the imagination, and they both fled, followed by Otto, who thought he would see if any of his cronies were supping downstairs. Needless to say the proprietor did not wish for a general stampede, so the Archduke was seized and got somehow into his uniform. This escapade caused much comment, and for some time the restaurants were not patronised by fathers of families for fear of encountering this drunken lunatic in a condition of nudity.

A favourite pastime of Otto was to keep an ox without water for days and nights, and then allow it to drink to repletion and die in agony. Another time he forced his military servant to drink brandy until he was helpless, and then the Archduke poured the raw spirit down the throat of the poor man, who died soon afterward from the effect.

Otto's death was a horrible Nemesis which followed his evil life. He was ill for years with a loathsome disease; his nose fell off, his once handsome face became a skull, and at last he was taken to his castle to die. His wife, who had been living apart from him, returned to his roof and remained with him to the end. Marie Josepha's devotion and goodness must have made the closing days of the unhappy, forsaken sinner easier, and it is no wonder that the Emperor loves her, or that the common people look upon her as a saint.

The last journey of the Habsburgs takes them to the gloomy vault beneath the Capuchin Church at Vienna. There rows and rows of the dead rest upon stone slabs, life's fret and fever over; and only the tarnished crowns upon the padlocked coffins serve as a reminder of the rank and state of those who lie within ... The noise of the city is without. The hurrying feet of the passers-by are on a level with the windows which light the vault, but the

Habsburgs sleep undisturbed, although the evil which has been wrought by many of them lives again in their descendants.

Elizabeth's body is in the middle of the vault. Rudolph is by her side, and the vacant slab will one day receive the Emperor's coffin when death calls him to his well-earned rest. It is a place of ghosts, this tomb-chamber, and they throng around those who disturb their privacy. Young and old, the beautiful, the gallant, and the reckless, all are here, and Time's waves flow over them until their very names are almost forgotten.

On Christmas Eve (Elizabeth's birthday), on September 10th, her death day, and on that fatal 30th of January, when Rudolph's shuddering soul fled into space, Francis-Joseph comes to pray with his dead. Does he ever see the Empress as she stands beside him, white as the morning mist? And when a breath of cold wind drifts across the vault, does the Emperor know that upon it are borne the shades of Rudolph and the woman who perished with him on that winter morning when they found their own way of escape?

CHAPTER VII
THE MAD KING OF BAVARIA

The insanity of royal houses · Where madness lies · King Ludwig II
of Bavaria – A disappointment in love · A changed man · He turns
night into day · The King's castles · A mania for building · A dinner
party · The ghosts of the past · The Spirit of the Mountains · The
King shatters his glass · What the servants did · The descending
table · A hint to "hurry up" · "The Sea Gull" and "The Mountain
Eagle" · Elizabeth corresponds with the King · The winter garden
at Munich · Under the shadow of the "Himalayas" – A property
moon · A leaking lake · Queen Marie changes her rooms · Josephina
Schefzky · "Save me Lohengrin" · I see the "Himalayas" · A hungry
actor · Herr Kainz and the cutlets · King Ludwig's death · King Otto
· Another mad monarch · I see him at Nymphenburg · "All in a
garden fair" · Schloss Fürstenried · An animal existence –
A new era for Bavaria

The members of the Royal and Ducal Houses of Bavaria are, taken all round, certainly far more interesting and clever than the Habsburgs. The eccentricities of the Wittelsbachs sometimes develop into madness, but the difference between the two families is, that with the Habsburgs insanity usually shows itself in depravity, self-effacement, and common marriages, while in the case of the Wittelsbachs it transforms the sufferer into a romantic being who is quite above the banalities of everyday life, but who occasionally deteriorates and becomes a gross feeder. There has always been a strain of madness in the Royal House, and certain eccentricities in the Ducal line, but none of us have ever committed the glaring indiscretions of the Habsburgs.

I knew the late King Ludwig II very well, for when I was quite a tiny child he used often to come to Garatshausen to see my father, of whom he was very fond.

Ludwig became King at the age of eighteen, and was then somewhat despotic, very romantic, and excessively clever. The young monarch was engaged to my aunt, Princess Sophie of Bavaria, but the engagement only lasted for a short time owing to the intrigues of the Court *entourage*, who disliked the idea of the match.

The Master of the Horse, Count Holnstein, was a good-looking man, who was much trusted and liked by the King, but the Count became the tool of the *entourage*, and was persuaded to inveigle the Princess into a flirtation in order to arouse Ludwig's jealousy. The Court photographer, who was in the plot, took some rather "affectionate" photographs of the Count and the Princess, which were shown to the King by the usual well-meaning friend, with the natural result that Ludwig became highly suspicious of his *fiancée*. He kept putting the wedding off on some pretext or other, until my grandfather, Duke Maximilien, wrote to him and said he would not allow his daughter to be treated in such a manner. The King, driven into a corner by his prospective father-in-law, and incited by his scheming counsellors, decided definitely to break off the engagement. It was a great blow to Princess Sophie, for she loved Ludwig dearly, although some years afterwards she accepted the hand of the Duc d'Alençon.

After the termination of his love affair, for which he alone was to blame, the King slowly developed into a morose, moody creature, a victim to melancholia, and obsessed with a thorough dislike for women, although he admired the ideal woman who never disappoints or disillusions too trusting man.

His kindness changed into cruelty where his servants were concerned, and he upset the generally accepted scheme of life by turning night into day. The command performances which he attended alone in the empty theatre began at midnight and were often not over till five A.M. His favourite opera was *Parsival*, and, as nearly everybody knows, the world of music is for ever indebted to Ludwig for the unfailing support which he gave Wagner, at a time when few people acknowledged his genius.

The King never cared for Munich, but liked to stay in his beautiful castles of Neu-Schwanstein, Herrenchiemsee, and Linderhof, where he indulged in the building and planting manias always associated with Louis XIV. At Linderhof, Ludwig made for himself a blue grotto, which was an exact copy of the famous one at Capri. Herrenchiemsee was a miniature Versailles, and it was here, in the Galerie des Glaces, that the King gave his ghostly dinner parties, one of which he afterwards described to my aunt, who in turn narrated the incidents and the conversations to me, although not literally in the words which follow:

Shortly before midnight, the wonderful "Galerie" glowed with the soft light of many candles which turned the crystal candelabra into chains of glittering diamonds. The dinner-table, which was decorated with gold plate and exquisite glass and flowers, was laid for thirteen guests, and at five minutes before midnight King Ludwig entered the room to await their arrival.

When the clock struck twelve, the great doors were flung open, and the Groom of the Chambers announced - Queen Marie Antoinette. Ludwig came forward to receive her, and what did he see? A beautiful woman dressed in delicate satin, her powdered hair entwined with pearls and roses, and round her neck a thin blood-red line; for the King imagined that at his bidding the Queen's spirit resumed the earthly aspect which she wore during the gorgeous days at Versailles, together with the cruel mark of the guillotine.

Louis XIV, with flowing wig and suit of stiff gold-encrusted brocade came mincingly forward on high red heels to be welcomed by his host; then Mary, Queen of Scots, lovely in black velvet, with the crimson kiss of death on her neck, looked deep into the King's eyes and enthralled his soul.

Catherine the Great, resplendent in her gorgeous robes, brought with her the taint of blood and desire, and the romantic troubadour Wolfram von Eschenbach, who followed the august lady, shivered as his sleeve inadvertently brushed her arm.

Julius Cæsar, whose bald head was encircled with a laurel wreath, entered with the all-conquering Alexander, and the

Emperor Constantine followed them absorbed by his vision of the Cross.

Hamlet, Prince of Denmark and the cross-grained cynic Diogenes seemed entirely out of place in that lovely glittering room, and so did the Emperor Barbarossa as he roughly acknowledged Ludwig's salutation. A solemn monk was the next arrival, and then the King looked anxious, for one guest was late, but at last the Spirit of the Mountains drifted lightly into the room. She was fair as the dawn which is only seen to perfection in the lonely places of the world, and her eyes were the deep blue of the quiet lakes. From beneath a crown of icicles her long fair hair fell over her white shoulders, and her transparent draperies were adorned with flowers and moss.

The King smiled at the Fairy, who kissed him with cold sweet lips that whispered of the purity of life far from the haunts of men; then she placed her hand upon his brow and bade him think of the forests, and the wild creatures which he loved and whose lives he held sacred.

Dinner was served, and thirteen servants waited on the guests, whose conversation was varied and often brilliant, as befitted such a gathering of the Great Ones of all Ages. But the Mountain Fairy sat by the King, and spoke of her distant home where the streams flowed swiftly over the emerald water weeds; she told him the secret which the wind tells the pine-trees in the dreary winter days, and how their resinous tears in summer are shed by the dryads imprisoned in their hearts. She made him smell the perfume of the flower-starred moss which she wore, and the enchanted King paid little attention to Marie Antoinette, who was talking trivialities about the Trianon and the Fountains of Versailles.

Finally Ludwig pledged his guests, and when the hands of the great gilt clock marked the hour of one he shattered his glass so that it could never be used to drink less noble toasts. Then silently and swiftly the ghostly diners disappeared, followed by the King.

Ludwig firmly imagined that this dinner was really attended by the illustrious dead, and his servants heightened the illusion by devouring the courses as soon as they were removed; so when the King passed through the serving room and saw that the food had really been consumed, he was more than ever convinced of the truth of his delusion.

Herrenchiemsee was never completed, as there was not sufficient money to carry out the King's grandiose schemes, but it was a lovely place even in its unfinished condition.

At Neu-Schwanstein the King would allow no servants to wait on him, and when he pressed a spring his round dinner-table sank through a hole in the floor; the next course was then set, and the table ascended into the dining-room again. Plenty of champagne in ice pails was placed near the King, and if the table did not return quickly enough he flung some bottles through the hole, as an emphatic reminder to the servants below that he objected to be kept waiting.

Sometimes at night (doubtless at the fancied bidding of the Spirit of the Mountains) the King would arouse his household in order to set out for one of his hunting-boxes, and peasants who heard the noise of his retinue passing in the dark shivered and crossed themselves, for they imagined that the Wild Huntsman and his ghostly hounds were abroad.

Elizabeth constantly wrote in verse to her cousin, and in this correspondence she was "the Sea-gull" and the King "the Mountain Eagle." The Empress was very fond of Ludwig, whose romanticism struck some corresponding chord in her own strange soul, and she never forgave the late Prince Regent for his share in the final tragedy which terminated Ludwig's existence.

The King had a wonderful winter garden at Munich, which was built on the roof of the Residenz. There was also an artificial lake with a painted panoramic background of the Himalaya Mountains, and when the King sat in the garden a "property" moon shed its gaseous light above the snow-capped peaks.

Queen Marie's bedroom was immediately under the winter garden, and one night the Queen, who was laid up with a heavy cold, was terrified out of her wits when she discovered that the lake was leaking through the ceiling, and that a slow but steady downpour was falling on her bed.

The unfortunate lady did not quite know what to do as she had been strictly enjoined by her doctors to keep in one temperature; she hastily summoned her attendants, however, and they brought a large umbrella under which she took shelter for two hours until the leakage was repaired. It is perhaps unnecessary to say that the Queen changed her rooms on the morrow and chose a part of the Residenz which was quite away from the danger zone.

The King used often to command artistes from the theatre to perform in the winter gardens and I remember the fate which befell Josephina Schefzky, a large, tall woman, whose one wish in life was to attract Ludwig's notice. As all the singers sang hidden behind screens, Josephina's chances of meeting the King face to face were exceedingly small; but what woman is ever at a loss for an expedient? She knew how chivalrously romantic Ludwig could be on occasions, so she decided that she would fall into the lake and entreat him to rescue her.

The eventful evening arrived, Josephina warbled her sweetest for the benefit of the listening monarch, and when the song was over plunged heavily into the lake.

There was a tremendous noise, and the water splashed to the topmost summit of the "Himalayas," but the lady remained chin-deep in the lake, whose still waters were not so deep as they looked. "Save me, save me, Lohengrin!" cried the agitated singer, but the King took not the slightest notice of her appeal.

He rang the bell. "Get that woman out of the lake and send her home," he commanded, and the dripping Josephina, sadder and wiser, walked out of the water and out of the Residenz for ever.

One day, when I was about fifteen, Ludwig and my father were discussing music, and when papa happened to remark that I had quite a nice voice the King instantly said that he would like to hear me sing. "It's a pity that the winter garden is disarranged, for then Marie could have sung to me there," observed Ludwig, a day or two later, when he had graciously expressed himself pleased with my efforts.

"Yes, indeed," I answered, "for I've always longed to see the beautiful garden."

The King said nothing, but the next day before he left Munich he sent for papa and told him that the winter garden had been put in order expressly for my benefit, and that we were all to go and see it that evening. It certainly was a pretty sight; the lake was very romantic; the moon rose without a hitch behind the pasteboard mountains, and when we returned home I was presented by the head gardener with a big bouquet of flowers in the King's name.

Ludwig had little consideration for the feelings of others; and I remember hearing a story about a clever actor, Joseph Kainz, who had been commanded to recite to him. Herr Kainz declaimed various pieces, but as the hours went by he began to feel hungry, and at last the sight of the King at dinner nearly drove him frantic.

Ludwig, who was blissfully unconscious of his ravenous subject, only heard the actor's sonorous voice reciting the poems he loved, and he was not prepared for what followed the arrival of a dish of cutlets.

Kainz stopped reciting, and hurried to where the King was seated. "For the love of Heaven give me a cutlet, Majestät," pleaded the actor in tragic accents - "I'm absolutely starving."

The King jumped up without saying a word and fled from the room. I do not know whether Herr Kainz profited by his absence and devoured the cutlets, but I do know that he was never asked to recite at the Residenz again.

There have been various rumours about King Ludwig's death, and it has been said that he was assassinated at the instigation of Bismarck; but as a member of the family I can most emphatically state that this was not the case. The King's madness assumed such a grave aspect that it became absolutely necessary to put him under restraint. However, he was quite sensible enough to understand what the loss of liberty would mean to anyone like himself who had hitherto moved free as air, and he chose death as a means of escape, and perhaps it was the best thing for him. No one actually knows what happened on that last walk which he and his doctor took by the lake of Starnberg, but in the morning when the dead bodies were found, the King was holding the doctor down under the water, and there is no doubt that a struggle had taken place.

Ludwig II died on June 13, 1886, and was succeeded by his brother Otto, whom I remember years ago in Munich as a good-natured, nice looking young man who used to come to our box at the opera. His mental trouble commenced when he returned from travelling in the East, where he had acquired a most distressing malady. Poor Otto used to get violent attacks of cramp, and it was most painful to see him at the theatre, as his complaint frequently forced him to scratch his hands until he drew blood.

Otto also suffered from fits, and was kept quite in the background at Nymphenburg where papa used to go and see him. One day I accompanied my father and sat down to wait in a little private garden until the visit was over. Suddenly I heard the sound of footsteps, and to my intense dismay I saw Otto standing before me; he looked dreadfully ill, and was changed almost beyond recognition, for his hair had grown long, and his nails were like claws. To my great surprise he recognised me, and said kindly, "Do you like flowers, Marie?"

"Very much indeed," I answered, wondering what would happen next.

Otto instantly began to uproot all the available plants, which he laid in a heap at my feet. I was very nervous and looked anxiously round to discover some way of escape, but luckily at that moment his attendant appeared and took him away.

The King now lives in retirement at Schloss Fürstenried, which is surrounded by a large deer park and is about two hours' drive from Munich.* Before he became hopelessly insane, his mother the late Queen Marie often used to visit him, but he is like an animal now and leads the existence of one. The late Prince Regent always insisted on every care being taken of his unfortunate nephew, and no doubt his son the present Regent is equally considerate; but with the death of the maniac-monarch and the accession of Prince Ludwig to the throne a new and happier royal era should begin for Bavaria.

* He was deposed in 1913 because of mental incapacity, and died in 1916.

CHAPTER VIII
ROYAL MISMATINGS

*My aunts - Women of temperaments - Queen Sophia of Naples -
Married by proxy – The King who was sick - "The heroine of Gaeta"
- The Rothschilds - 'Le bon sang ne peut pas mentir" - Princess
Thurn and Taxis - "Spatz" - The late Duchesse d'Alençon –
She prays beside King Ludwig's coffin - "Do you think he has
forgiven me?" – My grandparents - Their marriage - Locked in - A
black beginning - Princess Alexandra - Another mad member of the
family - Dust - The sofa - A journey to Vienna –
The beautiful bonnet from Bavaria - An upset - What happened to
the hat-box – The Empress at Bad Kreuth - A startling story -
Water everywhere - King Ludwig appears to my aunt - "She burns
in torment" - "You will join us" - The Empress is convinced about
the truth of her story - The woman who was burnt –
Did Ludwig really return? – Secret sympathy*

My aunts were all charming women of varied temperaments, although they had a strong facial resemblance to one another.

Queen Sophia of Naples* lives principally in Munich and is much liked by most people with whom she comes in contact. She was married by proxy at the age of fifteen, and was greatly disappointed when she arrived at Naples and saw her husband for the first time, as the portrait which had been sent for her inspection had depicted a very handsome man, whereas the King was chiefly remarkable for his ugliness. My aunt, who was both philosophical and courageous, managed to conceal her chagrin, but I think the unforeseen contretemps which occurred on her wedding night thoroughly disgusted her with her husband.

* Better remembered as Queen Maria Sophia, she died in 1925.

The young bride was duly put to bed, with much ceremony, by her ladies-in-waiting, and after King Francis had joined her, the bedroom doors were locked and the keys were taken away by a high official. Unfortunately the King had over-eaten himself at the State banquet, and in consequence was violently ill nearly the whole night. As there were no bells in the bedchamber, the unpleasant state of things which confronted the officials next morning when they unlocked the doors may be well imagined.

My aunt was very unhappy, for King Francis was a despicable creature, who had not one taste or sympathy in common with his wife, and his death must have come as a positive relief to her.

Queen Sophia has been called "The heroine of Gaeta," in recognition of the courage she displayed in connection with the defence of the city when it was besieged by the army of King Victor Emmanuel. It might almost be asserted that she conducted the entire defence herself, and the brave garrison were allowed to march out with all the honours of war. The Queen visited the ramparts and even helped to sight the guns.

I remember Aunt Sophia told me that she was attended during the siege by an old Italian Duchess who was devoted to her, but who was so scared when the firing commenced that she spent most of the time crouched underneath her bed.

After the war the King and Queen lived in Rome for some years, where their only child died. When I was quite a girl I spent two months with Aunt Sophia at St. Mandé, where she had a villa. While there I was often taken to see the Paris Rothschilds, and made the acquaintance of Bettina Rothschild, one of the most charming of women, who, curiously enough, did not possess any of the pronounced Hebraic facial characteristics of the illustrious family of the "Red Shield."

My aunt, Princess Hélène, whom Francis-Joseph deliberately jilted in order to marry her younger sister Elizabeth, became the consort of Prince Thurn and Taxis, who was the richest Prince in Bavaria. It was a loveless union, and after her husband's death the Princess became *devoté*, and ultimately developed religious mania. When Aunt Hélène died the Empress took charge of her eldest son Max, and a great affection existed between them, but my cousin died when he was quite a young man, and his brother, who married the Archduchess Marguerite, is now head of the house.

Princess Mathilde, my father's third sister, married Prince Trani, brother of the King of Naples. She is best described as having been a caricature of the Empress; like Elizabeth, she understood the art of dress, and her excessive thinness earned for her in the family the nickname of "Spatz" (sparrow).

The late Duchesse d'Alençon was a sweet soul whose heroic death was quite in keeping with her saintly life. My aunt never really recovered from the shock of her broken engagement with King Ludwig, and was always a saddened woman. I remember I was staying at Munich when she came there after the King's death, and she asked me if I would go with her into the crypt, as she wished to pray beside the dead. The Duchess carried a beautiful wreath, tied with purple ribbons, which she placed on the coffin, and then knelt down and cried as if her heart would break. I let her grief subside before I ventured to console her, because I felt that at such a moment words were useless. Suddenly my aunt looked at me, and said in tones of indescribable pathos: "Oh! Marie, do you think he has forgiven me?"

The marriage of my grandparents was, like most of the family's matrimonial ventures, somewhat of a failure, and the ceremony took place at Schloss Tegernsee, the summer residence of the old King Max Joseph I. My grandmother, who was a tall, handsome girl, objected to her short, plain husband, but as she had been commanded to marry Duke Max, she had to make the best of him.

Tegernsee, which was formerly a convent, is a curious old place full of long passages, where little doors open into the numerous stove-rooms which supply the castle with heat.

There was none of the ceremony of undressing the bride which characterised the nuptials of the Queen of Naples. My grandparents walked unattended down the corridor which led to their bridal chamber, and my grandmother's aversion to her husband suddenly became so acute that she decided she could not and would not allow him to share her room that night. A happy thought seized her as they passed one of the half-open doors; the bride expressed some curiosity to know what was inside, so the bridegroom obligingly went to investigate, and, once inside, my grandmother locked him in, put the key in her pocket, and ran away. Next morning a frightened servant reported that there was an unearthly noise in the passage, and sure enough a muffled sound of knocking and swearing was heard when a search party arrived on the scene. After some hesitation a bold spirit unlocked the door of the stove-room whence the sounds proceeded, and to the consternation of every one the sooty figure which emerged proved to be none other than the Duke, who by rights should have been in far more comfortable surroundings.

After this black beginning of their married life, it is hardly surprising that my grandparents were not on the best of terms, and during the last years of their lives, although they lived under the same roof, they rarely met.

My father has often told me an amusing experience which happened to him when he went with my grandmother to Vienna on the occasion of Elizabeth's marriage to Francis-Joseph. There were no railways in those days, so the long journey was made in four great post carriages. The first contained my grandmother, Princess Elizabeth, and a lady-in-waiting; my father, the Court Chamberlain, and two officials occupied the second, whilst the other carriages were filled with servants and luggage.

My grandmother had bought a wonderful new bonnet with which she intended to pulverise the Viennese, and, fearful lest anything should befall it, she entrusted it to my father, who nursed the enormous box containing it the whole way.

Just before they reached Vienna, my father's carriage was upset, and in the confusion which ensued he unluckily sat on the box and went through the lid. "My bonnet, my bonnet!" shrieked his dismayed mother, who had hastily left her carriage to see what had happened.

"It is quite safe," exclaimed papa; and as he spoke he placed the damaged headgear on his knee and tried to arrange its ruffled plumage; but the straw was weak, and his pushing and contriving sent his knee right through the crown and ruined it beyond redemption. My grandmother was furious, and during the whole of her stay in Vienna she never ceased to lament that people had not been able to admire the beautiful bonnet from Bavaria.

The late Regent's sister, Princess Alexandra, was very mad indeed, and gossip attributed this to an unhappy love-affair. She was devoted to a young officer, but the bare idea of such a marriage was regarded as impossible, and the lovely girl became morose and moody, like King Ludwig under similar circumstances.

The particular mania which possessed the Princess was the delusion that she was covered with dust; so she and her clothes were brushed all day by relays of maids, and even her food and drink had to be dusted before her eyes. Another of her odd delusions was that a sofa had taken up its permanent abode in her head, and the Princess considered that it was most dangerous for her to go through a door in case she knocked the ends of the sofa. This awkward state of things was happily put an end to, for some master-mind hit upon the idea of placing a doll's sofa in the basin which was used when the Princess had a bilious attack, and she was told that her sufferings had been occasioned by the sofa's struggles for freedom, which were now at an end owing to its fortunate escape from her mouth.

In 1887, the year after King Ludwig's death, I went to stay at Bad Kreuth, near Tegernsee, where the Empress joined me; Elizabeth had not seen me since the tragic occurrence at Lake Starnberg, and we discussed the King and many incidents of his life about which we alone knew the truth.

One day we took a long walk, and the conversation turned as usual on Ludwig. We had sat down to rest, and perhaps the lonely grandeur of the mountains by which we were surrounded recalled our dead cousin to us.

"He is not happy," said Aunt Cissi, and the mystic look deepened in her eyes as she spoke. "I frequently speak to Ludwig, and his soul has *not* found peace."

I was well accustomed to Elizabeth's strange ideas, and did not express any astonishment, but only asked, "Have you seen the King?"

"Yes, Marie," answered my aunt. "Listen, for what I am about to tell you is perfectly true. The first night that I slept in Bavaria after Ludwig's death he appeared to me."

"Oh, Aunt Cissi, surely it was a dream?"

"It was no dream," replied the Empress. "I had gone to bed, but I could not sleep, although the room was in darkness and everything outside was perfectly still.

"As I lay awake in the lonely hours thoughts assailed me, and suddenly I fancied I heard a monotonous drip, drip, of water.

"'It must be raining,' I said to myself, 'and the drops are falling on the leaves close to my window,' so I took no further notice until the noise was succeeded by the unmistakable ripple of water when it kisses the shore.

"You know that sound, Marie. We have heard it often as we rode by Lake Starnberg. As the gentle, rippling sound continued it gradually filled the room, and I began to experience all the sensations of drowning. I choked and gasped as I struggled for air; but the terror passed, and with an effort I sat up in bed and breathed freely.

"The moon had now risen, and its radiance made the room as light as day. Then I saw the door open very slowly, and Ludwig came within.

"His clothes were heavy with water, which dripped from them and made little pools on the parquet. His damp hair lay close round his white face, but it was Ludwig much as he had looked in life.

"We gazed at each other in silence, and then the King said slowly and sadly:

"'Cissi, are you frightened of me?'

"'No, Ludwig, I am not frightened.'

"'Ah me!' he sighed. 'Death has not brought me peace. Cissi, *she* burns in torment. The flames encircle her, the smoke suffocates her. She burns and I am powerless to save her.'

"'*Who* burns, dear cousin?' I asked.

"'I do not know because her face is hidden,' he answered, 'but I know that it is a woman who loved me, and until her destiny is fulfilled I shall not be free. But afterwards you will join us and we three shall be happy in Paradise together.'

"'What do you mean? When shall I follow you?'

"'I cannot tell you *when*,' replied Ludwig, 'for in the abode of earth-bound souls time has no place.'

"'By which road shall I join you? Will it be a journey of painful old age, hampered by regrets and recollections?'

"'No, Cissi,' said my cousin; 'you will shed many tears, and experience both regrets and recollections before you come to us, but your journey will be swift, and you will have no warning of it.'

"'Shall I suffer?'

"He smiled. 'No, you will *not* suffer.'

"'How do I know that I am not dreaming?' I asked.

"Ludwig slowly came to my bedside, and oh! Marie, the coldness of death and the grave was in the air. 'Give me your hand,' he said.

"I put out my hand, and his wet fingers closed over mine. At that moment all my pity sprang into life. 'Ah stay,' I pleaded, 'do not leave the friend who loves you to return to your sufferings. Oh, Ludwig, pray with me for peace.' But as I spoke the figure vanished, and again I heard the drip of the invisible water succeeded by the ripple of the lake among the reeds. Panic seized me, for I felt I was very near the dwellers in that other world who stretch out their shadowy arms and beseech consolation from the living.

"Then I became unconscious, and must have fallen asleep. When I awoke the dawn was in the sky, but I knew then, as I know now, that I had actually seen and talked with Ludwig."

"Who could he have meant by the woman who burns?" I asked.

"I cannot imagine," replied Aunt Cissi.

The Empress often spoke about her strange experience, and when the Duchesse d'Alençon perished in the awful fire at the Charity Bazaar, I am told Elizabeth declared to others that Ludwig's words were fulfilled, and that she must prepare for the last journey, which she was destined to take a year and four months after her sister's death.

Many people will doubtless ridicule this story, which I wrote down at the time, and which I give almost exactly in the Empress's own words, but those who believe that sympathy between souls can exist beyond the grave will not deem it improbable that Elizabeth and Ludwig met once more.

It is the secret sympathy,
The silver link, the silver tie,
Which heart to heart, and mind to mind
In body and in soul can bind.

*Ludwig Wilhelm and Henriette, Duke and Duchess in Bavaria,
and their daughter Marie, c.1872*

Empress Elizabeth, c.1865

Countess Marie Larisch and her cousin Archduchess Valerie,
youngest daughter of Empress Elizabeth, c.1878

Emperor Francis Joseph, c.1878

Count Georg Larisch von Moennich, c.1878

Countess Marie Larisch, c.1880

Crown Prince Rudolf, c.1886

Ludwig II, King of Bavaria

Marie Vetsera, 1887

Countess Larisch and Marie Vetsera, 1888

Crown Prince Rudolf and Crown Princess Stéphanie

The hunting lodge at Mayerling

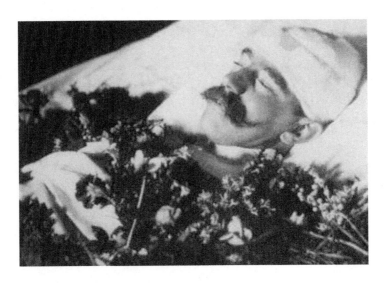

Crown Prince Rudolf after death

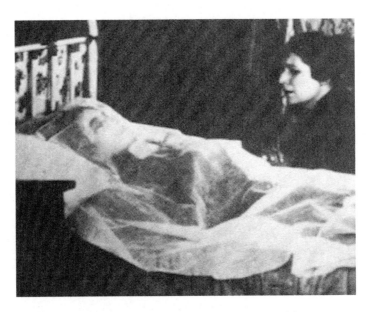

*A surviving fragment from the film based around
the death of Empress Elizabeth, 1921*

CHAPTER IX
THE INFATUATION OF MARY VETSERA

Drifting into dullness - A quiet life - My accident - Aunt Cissi comes to see me – Her conversation with me - Blood and tears - The month which brought about my destiny - The drama of Mayerling - I speak after twenty-four years' silence - I meet the Baroness Vetsera in Vienna - The family history - The Baltazzis - A popular hostess – I lunch at the Vetsera Palace - A quarrel - "Mary dear" - Her beauty - Her hero-worship - Mary's letter - To whom did she write? - I hear the whole story - A midnight meeting – I give Mary some unwelcome advice - She will not listen

Since that October day when, solely to please the Empress, I became the wife of Count George Larisch, my life was more or less uneventful. My husband's sudden self-assertion had shattered Elizabeth's plans, and, although I saw a great deal of her when I, happened to be in Vienna, the confidential intercourse between us was practically over, and I sometimes bitterly reflected that my aunt did not seem to trouble about me or my affairs half so much as when I was more useful to her.

The Count and I first lived in a remote part of Silesia, and we afterwards removed to another estate near where my husband's people resided. George was not on the best of terms with his relations, and he therefore decided to purchase a property in Bohemia, not far from Pardubitz, where he built a country house. I did not care greatly for our new home, which bored me excessively when the hunting and shooting were over, but luckily I owned a charming little place in the Bavarian mountains where I spent some very happy times with my children.

Count Larisch did not give us much of his company in Bavaria, as he had a deep-rooted dislike to my country, and to my family;

so his visits to the Villa Valérie only lasted a few weeks. But I was not actually unhappy; I loved my children; I had many things to occupy my time, and perhaps a little of the stolid Bavarian character made me philosophical. I had, like most women, some one for whom I cared, but this was my own secret, and the object of my affection knew nothing about it. I drifted peacefully through the days which were so much alike; I never expected any change, for my emotions had become dulled, and I had schooled myself to accept my life such as it was.

In 1886 I met with a bad accident when I was riding in the Empress's private exercising ground. My horse came down with me, and the pommel broke my ribs. I hurt my eyes and nose, my teeth were loosened, and for six weeks I lay helpless in a darkened room. Aunt Cissi was very kind to me then, and often came to sit with me, and, as of old, she fascinated me and I felt some of my former great affection for her.

Elizabeth was just beginning to be wrapped in her dreams of Ancient Greece, and she seemed to have put away the lighter things of life and to find consolation in more serious subjects. One day I reproached her for having sacrificed me to suit her own purposes.

"My dear Marie," she answered, "I cannot help being selfish; my training has made me so; people put themselves at my disposal, why should I not make use of them?"

"It was not quite kind to take me away from my life at Munich," I said bitterly.

"You belonged to me since that day at Garatshausen," she replied. "You saw me weep, and no one but you has ever seen my tears. If you are disappointed with life, so am I, because I consider it has treated me most unfairly. Why do you not take refuge in the sanctuary of your soul, where you can make peace for yourself and rest secure from the petty ills which assail the restless mind?"

I pointed out that it was not possible for Marie Larisch to live in the unreal world which Elizabeth of Austria had discovered for herself, and that I could not find happiness in such an existence.

"I have a strange presentiment that your life is about to change," observed Aunt Cissi, suddenly but thoughtfully;

"sometimes I see you in the midst of blood and tears, and I hear voices which tell me to beware of the future."

"But you will always be my friend?" I inquired.

"*Always*, so long as I am not deceived in you," replied Elizabeth.

"You have hitherto found me worthy of your trust and friendship," I reminded her.

"Oh - as to trust - yes," said Aunt Cissi. "There is no such thing as friendship; it is a broken reed which can never be relied upon when real trouble comes. Poets sing its pure joys, but believe me no action done in the name of friendship ever yet sprang from a disinterested motive. It is a farce between men and women, since no man ever yet assisted a woman without believing that what he gave she would eventually return to him in kind."

"You have strange thoughts," I said, "and your ideas frighten me."

The Empress was silent, but I could not help thinking over what she said, and I devoutly prayed that a future filled with blood and tears was not to be my portion.

In September, 1888, I came to Vienna, happily ignorant that destiny would soon compel me to play an unwilling part in a tragedy which is always considered to be one of the greatest mysteries of our time.

There have been many accounts written of the drama of Mayerling. Various people have asserted that they alone know the truth. So-called eye-witnesses have given their versions of the affair, and a tissue of lies has been woven around me in connection with the deaths of my cousin, the Crown Prince Rudolph of Austria, and the Baroness Mary Vetsera. Hitherto I have not refuted the slanders circulated about me, as I deemed them unworthy of notice. But as one of my sons shot himself on account of what he read in one of the lying books, and my daughters' lives have been embittered by hearing so much that is untrue regarding the part I played in the drama, I have made up my mind to speak after a silence of twenty-four years and acquaint the world with the truth of what really happened before and after the tragedy of Mayerling.

The month of September, 1888, was one of those delicious afterthoughts of summer, and I was thoroughly enjoying a week's shopping in Vienna. I was staying at the Grand Hotel, and had not told anyone of my arrival, as I did not wish to be bothered with invitations to lunch and dinner. One morning when I was walking on the "Ring" I suddenly heard my name pronounced, and turning round I encountered the Baroness Vetsera.

The Baroness was a very small woman, whose ultra-smart gowns disguised her ill-proportioned, slightly humpbacked figure, but she was really handsome notwithstanding these defects, and her expressive dark grey eyes would have made any face beautiful.

"Oh, Marie, how glad I am to see you!" she exclaimed. "What brings you to Vienna?"

"New clothes," I answered laconically; "that's to say, the want of them, but I am only here *en passant*."

"Are you alone?"

"Absolutely."

"Then I will take no refusal. Come and lunch with us. Mary and Hannah are at home, and you know how delighted 'Mary dear' will be to see you. You *will* come?"

I hesitated: "You will be quite *en famille*?"

"Quite," answered the Baroness, "and I shall go back at once and tell the girls they are to expect you."

She gave me a friendly handshake and I continued my walk. I rather liked the Baroness, although Count Larisch rudely termed the whole family *rastaquouères*. All smart Vienna went to the Vetsera Palace, and if the women said horrid things about their hostess they enjoyed her dinner-parties, for she was a thoughtful and tactful woman, who contrived that her guests should always be asked to meet the very people they desired to see.

The Baroness Vetsera's father, Herr Baltazzi, originally came from Constantinople, where he had occupied a responsible position in the house of an influential pasha. After the pasha's death Baltazzi went to England, where he married, and afterwards he and his children settled in Austria.

As the boys were sportsmen, and the girls pretty and fascinating, the Baltazzis, who spent their money freely, were at once welcomed by Viennese society. Evelyn Baltazzi married Count George Stockau, her sister, Marie-Virginia ("Bibi"), married Count St. Julien, and Hélène became the wife of Baron Vetsera, by whom she had four children - Hannah, Mary, and two sons, Lazlo and Féry.

The Baltazzi brothers, Alexandre, Hector, Aristide, and Henri, were all charming, somewhat Oriental-looking men, and although the family never went to Court, the Emperor and Empress showed them great kindness, and, as I have before mentioned, Elizabeth herself introduced me to the Baroness.

Madame Vetsera's reputation was not what is usually termed "good," but the Viennese aristocracy are most tolerant of flirtations, and much is forgiven a woman who spends money in lavishly entertaining other people. I saw a good deal of the Vetseras from time to time, and "Mary dear" - for so she was called by her friends - was greatly attached to me. The whole family went to Cairo in the winter of 1887, on account of the Baron's ill-health, and from there I received most romantic and indiscreet letters from Mary, who had a love-affair with an English officer. When she returned to Vienna, in March, 1888, after her father's death, Mary was no longer the innocent girl she had been. She told me all about the young officer when we met, and rather lamented that his lack of money and prospects had prevented a marriage between them.

I arrived at the Vetsera Palace about half an hour before luncheon, and as I wanted to have a little chat with Hannah and Mary, I walked unannounced to the girls' rooms.

As I softly opened the door, I heard the sound of angry voices, and when I got inside the room I heard Mary say something which evidently irritated her sister.

Hannah Vetsera, a quiet, reserved, plain-looking girl, was engaged in her favourite occupation of painting. Her room opened into Mary's, and they had obviously had a sharp quarrel, for Hannah looked angry and disturbed.

"Well, Mary dear!" I said.

At the sound of my voice, a young girl who was bending over a writing-table looked up, and when she saw who it was, threw herself into my arms and kissed me over and over again.

The image of Mary Vetsera is unfading in my remembrance, and I have only to close my eyes to see her in all the freshness of her beauty. She was not tall, and her supple figure and well-developed bust made her look older than her eighteen years. Her complexion was lovely, and her red, voluptuous mouth parted over sharp little white teeth, which I used to call her "mouse-teeth." Mary's nose was slightly *retroussé*, but it gave an added piquancy to her lovely face, and I have never seen such beautiful eyes as she possessed - deep blue, with curling lashes set off by finely-marked eyebrows. Her dark brown hair was very long, she had nice hands and feet, and she walked with a seductive, swaying grace that was irresistible.

"Oh, Marie, I'm *so* glad to see you," she said between her kisses.

"Gently, gently," I answered. "Why, what's the matter? Your eyes don't look in the least kind, and your cheeks are red. I'm sure you and Hannah have been quarrelling."

"Mary is a stupid child," announced Hannah from the adjoining room. "I think she is fast losing what little sense she has."

"I am not," retorted Mary angrily.

"Whatever is the matter?" I demanded.

"Well," said Hannah, laying down her brush, and coming into her sister's room, "I'll tell you, and you will never believe Mary could be so foolish. Fancy, she is madly in love with ... now ... I'll break this to you *very* gently - she is in love with the Crown Prince! Oh, Marie, you can't imagine anything so silly, and she has no idea how ridiculous it is."

Mary's eyes blazed, but she made no reply. Hannah continued, "All the love she has for you is solely on account of your being Rudolph's cousin, and she thinks you resemble him: do tell her what he eats and drinks, for it will interest her *so* much."

"And whose concern is it if I choose to admire the Crown Prince?" asked Mary with languid insolence. "It is a pleasure to adore anyone who is so totally different from other men; I know a great deal about him already from Miguel Braganza."

"Yes, you talked nothing else but Rudolph, and the poor man was nearly worn out with your questions," observed Hannah.

At this moment a servant announced that luncheon was served, and the altercation was fortunately terminated. I was surprised to see that the Baroness seemed fully aware of Mary's hero-worship, which she treated as a great joke; but knowing her daughter's impulsive nature I was glad to think it was not likely she would ever encounter Rudolph in private life.

What a strange creature Mary was! She was a coquette by instinct, unconsciously unmoral in her tendencies, almost Oriental in her sensuous ideas, but withal so sweet and lovable that she was a favourite with every one. She was amorous by nature, and her Egyptian episode had transformed her from a girl into a woman who already knew the meaning of passion.

Mary's mind had unfortunately been corrupted by improper books, which her maid Agnes had surreptitiously procured for her, and many of her ideas of love and lovers were derived from immoral and highly coloured French novels.

After luncheon Mary carried me off to her room, and once there she literally bombarded me with questions about my cousin. I was rather amused, for I never imagined him as the kind of man who would captivate the fancy of a young girl.

"Marie dear, I wish you would do something for me," she pleaded, as she rested her pretty head on my shoulder.

"Well ... what is it, you silly girl?" I questioned.

"You are going to the festivities for your grandparents' diamond wedding," she answered. "I know Rudolph will be there. Do tell him that some one who loves him sends him an affectionate greeting."

"I'll do nothing of the kind," I replied. "My dear child, wolves like Rudolph only eat up little lambs like you. I assure you he is not really the hero you imagine him to be, but a I rather heartless and fast man."

"I won't believe it," she exclaimed. "At any rate do give him my message." But I would not listen to any more of her nonsense, and when I bade her good-bye, I looked her full in the face, and said: "Now when I come back to Vienna, I hope to hear that you have put Rudolph out of your mind. Believe me, 'Mary dear,' he's not worth serious consideration."

I soon forgot Mary Vetsera's affairs, but on my return to Vienna for a few days' stay, I received a letter from her asking if she could come to tea one afternoon. I sent word that I should be delighted, and in due course Mary and her maid arrived at the hotel.

I quite expected to hear Rudolph's name the first moment we were alone, but to my great surprise Mary did not refer to him, but instead she told me all the Vienna gossip, and I was pleased to fancy that her infatuation for my cousin was at an end.

Before leaving, Mary asked permission to write a letter which she afterwards slipped into her sealskin muff, and begged me to come down to the carriage with her. "Just for a last kiss," she explained.

As I bade her good-bye, I was surprised to see her suddenly dart to the hotel post-box and drop in the letter she had written upstairs; then she gave me another hurried kiss and was gone.

The next day I received a note from Mary. "*Do* let me come and see you this evening," she wrote. "I've a great deal to tell you." As I was quite alone I was not averse to seeing her, so I wrote to the Baroness and asked if Mary could spend the evening with me.

She was in high spirits that night, and danced about the room, kissing me at intervals until, grown calmer, she sat down beside me.

"Can you keep a very, very, great secret, Marie?" she asked.

I smiled, as I thought whose secrets I had kept once upon a time. "I believe I can," I said.

"Without *ever* telling anyone ?"

"*Without ever telling anyone.*"

"Then listen. Now Marie, let me hold your hand tight - how kind you are, so ... now I'll begin. I know Rudolph *at last*. I couldn't live without him, he filled my thoughts, I *had* to tell him all I felt."

I started. What was I going to hear next? But all I could say at the moment was, "Well, Mary?"

"I wrote to him," she continued. "I told him that I loved him, and that my greatest wish was to speak to him. Could he grant me an interview? A letter sent to the Poste Restante under a number would reach me."

"And Rudolph?" I queried, still wondering whether I was asleep or awake.

"Rudolph wrote," replied Mary. "He told me that every night at twelve o'clock a fiacre would wait for an hour in the Salesianergasse, so if I had the chance to get out I should know exactly what to do."

"Had he any idea from your letter who you were?" I asked.

"I think so," she answered, "for he has often stared at me when I have seen him driving in the Prater."

"Surely in the name of fortune you were never so imprudent as to meet my cousin?"

"Oh, don't look so shocked, Marie."

"I *am* shocked. Tell me at once."

"Well ... yes - I went."

I was thunderstruck, for I knew how strictly Mary was kept, and that she was not even allowed to go the length of the street unattended.

"I took Agnes into my confidence," explained Mary. "She was the best person to tell, all things considered, because, as her father is the concierge at our place, it is easy for her to get the keys from him whenever I want to go out and come in unperceived."

I did not care for Agnes, who was generally supposed to have been rather free in her behaviour with all the men of the Baltazzi family, and I told Mary that I considered her conduct most reprehensible.

She laughed and lit a cigarette. Then she continued her story. "I *did* get out - I put a dressing-gown over my nightdress, and once safely past Hannah, who sleeps like the dead, I crept downstairs. There Agnes was waiting with my long coat and a thick veil in which I muffled my head and face. She unlocked the door, and I ran down the street and jumped into the fiacre, which was waiting just where Rudolph had said."

"And then?"

"Then we drove off, and a little while after the fiacre stopped. A figure came out of the night. It was Rudolph! Ah, Marie, how can I express my feelings? I almost fainted with joy when I knew he was actually by my side. That drive was heaven to me. We talked of so many things, and he was just as adorable as I had imagined him."

"Oh, Mary, Mary," I said. "Poor child – *do* think what you are doing, for such an intrigue will never have any good results."

She flung her arms round me. "You will not betray us?"

"No, no," I said, "it has nothing to do with me - besides I don't want to be dragged into such a mad adventure."

Mary was at evident pains to assure me that the affair was quite innocent. Viewed through her eyes the Crown Prince's morals were unimpeachable. I was rather incredulous, for I had never heard Rudolph spoken of as a man who respected youth and innocence when once his desires were in question.

"I know it is only a happy dream," she continued, "from which I shall have an awakening one day, and then I shall marry some one else. I've even spoken to Rudolph about the person who would like to make me his wife."

I was quite interested and asked who was the prospective fiancé.

"It is that silly Duke of Braganza," laughed. Mary. "He knows all about my affair with the Crown Prince."

"Indeed," I said, "and do you honestly believe that knowing all about it he will marry you?"

"He is so much in love with me that he will do anything I wish. You know how stupid he is."

Mary's cynicism rather repelled me. "Listen," I said, "take my advice, and drop this flirtation with Rudolph; it is dangerous, and once people get to know about it, not even your easy-going Miguel will marry you when the affair becomes a public scandal. ... However we won't discuss it," and I changed the conversation. She was tactful enough not to refer to the subject, but when she bade me good-night, Mary said simply: "You will keep my secret, Marie?"

"Yes; I've already promised," I replied. "You know my opinion of your behaviour, and you know how Rudolph can compromise you."

Mary had become nervous and irritable, but I did not spare her feelings. "You will also have the Crown Princess to reckon with," I continued, "and I assure you she can be a most bitter enemy, so - all things considered - I do not think much of your prospects of happiness. And don't forget there is also the Empress. What would she think?"

"What would *she* think?" retorted Mary contemptuously. "As if the Empress ever thought of anything or anybody except herself."

CHAPTER X
THE PROGRESS OF AN AMOUR

*Pardubitz - No news of Mary - I do not treat her love affair seriously
- My explanation of the reason Why? - "Qui s'excuse, s'accuse" - I
return to Vienna - Luncheon at the Vetsera Palace - A drive in the
Prater - We meet the Crown Prince - I discover I have been made a
fool of - I tell Mary what I think of her behaviour - She confides in
me - A strange character - We go to the Opera - The wife and the
mistress - Angry glances - I am in for a bad quarter of an hour - The
fatal photograph - "True till death" – Christmas in the country -
Count Larisch decides to go to the Riviera - His opinion of Mary –
"Oh, George, how dense you are"*

I stayed some weeks at Pardubitz, and heard nothing from Mary.
The open-air life filled up my time, and I cannot honestly say that
I troubled myself very much about what she was doing. As this
attitude of mine may, perhaps, give rise to unfavourable comment,
I think I had better explain that other people's love affairs have
never interested me greatly, and that I did not regard Mary's
infatuation as being likely to involve her in serious consequences.
Looking at the whole matter in a perfectly impersonal light, I
suppose the right thing for me to have done was to have
acquainted Madame Vetsera at once with what I knew; but I
refrained from doing so, because I had no conviction that Mary
was seriously in love with Rudolph, and I had also pledged my
word that I would not reveal what she had told me.

The first frosts soon put an end to the hunting, and as I was
having trouble with my teeth I decided to return to Vienna.

Count Larisch raised no objection when I told him of my
intention. "All I ask of you, Marie, is not to see too much of the

Baltazzi crowd," he said, "and ... as for Madame Vetsera and Mary, I dislike the pair."

"My dear George," I replied coldly, "I am surely quite capable of choosing my own friends. You effectually interfered between Aunt Cissi and myself; please don't do so with the Baltazzis."

The interview with my dentist resulted in the knowledge that I should be obliged to stay in Vienna longer than I had at first intended. Almost everybody except the Vetseras was out of town, and as I was rather bored I got into the habit of dropping in to see them whenever I felt inclined.

Mary did not mention Rudolph, but she seemed nervous and overwrought, and I was sorry to notice the constant friction between her and Hannah. They were always bickering, and one day at lunch the sisters quarrelled openly, without paying the slightest attention to the presence of the Baroness or myself. At last Mary threw down her knife and fork, pushed her chair back from the table, and went out of the dining-room crying. Her mother followed her, and I had to listen to Hannah's angry outpourings about her sister. "If mamma were to do the sensible thing, she would thrash Mary," she said. "I'm sick to death of her; she is just a bundle of nerves, and ... "but the entrance of the Baroness put an end to Hannah's confidences.

"Mary is really not well," Madame Vetsera observed. "I wonder, Marie, if you would mind taking her out with you this afternoon; the poor child has an idea that she would like some fresh air."

Hannah shrugged her shoulders, and after luncheon, when I went to Mary's room, I found she had dried her tears and was all smiles and excitement.

"Dear - dear Marie, so you will take me? Oh, how angelic you are. Let us drive in the Prater at four o'clock - do say yes."

"What on earth happens in the Prater at four o'clock?"

Mary kissed me. "Why 'HE' often drives there, and I should love to catch a glimpse of him; there's no harm in it," she said anxiously, for she could see that I was not too well pleased. "You are so sympathetic that you will understand how miserable I am at home. I've not seen Rudolph for such a long time; now don't refuse this tiny favour, dear Marie."

It would have taken a much harder-hearted person than myself to refuse, and, after all, it seemed a small request.

"Well, I don't care much about it, but I'll go with you to the Prater," I answered; and Hannah, who had entered the room unperceived by us, said ironically:

"So the poor child wants to go to the Prater. Take her by all means, or else she will be ill again."

At four o'clock Mary and I found ourselves in the almost deserted avenue of the Prater. As I had brought my Scotch terrier in the carriage, I decided to get out and let him have a run directly we had seen the Crown Prince. We had not long to wait, for a phaeton soon came in sight, and as it passed I recognised Rudolph, who was driving himself. He gave us one look, but, as Mary behaved discreetly and took no notice, I was pleased, in a way, that I had been able to gratify her whim. "Don't let' Boy' get out here," she said; "let us drive on to the 'Étoile du Prater'; it is ever so much nicer there."

We left the carriage at the "Étoile," and I did not pay much attention when I heard Mary tell the man to wait for us behind the bridge; she then slipped her arm through mine, and we made our way towards the lonely shrubberies, greatly to "Boy's" delight.

"Now, we can talk quietly," said Mary. "I am just about as miserable as it is possible to be. Hannah nags at me the whole day and does her 'best to set mamma against me. ... I'm tired of my life," she added bitterly.

"Perhaps Hannah suspects more than she tells you," I observed. "Now, Mary, what are you and Rudolph doing? I hope that you have tired of this silly flirtation. What I dread is any gossip or scandal, for you are such an indiscreet, impulsive little girl."

Mary laughed cynically. "Oh, the gossip has started already, and that stupid Crown Princess knows I am her rival."

I was stupefied, and for a moment I made no reply. Mary looked lovely that autumn afternoon; her cheeks glowed like a vivid carnation, and she wore a chic grey costume with beautiful furs. I felt that Stéphanie would fully realise how dangerous this girl was, and I was certain she would be no sweet enemy when once her jealousy was aroused.

We had now reached the "wild" part of the Prater, which is like a wood intersected by numerous pathways, and I took the one which would eventually lead us back to the avenue where our carriage was waiting. Mary was behind me, as her garter wanted attention, and had disappeared out of observation to fasten it. I was keeping a sharp eye on "Boy," whose hunting instincts were much to the fore, for I did not want the little dog to meet with the fate which is reserved for poachers. At last I recollected Mary, but when I turned round, I discovered to my intense dismay that she was nowhere to be seen.

I called her, but got no reply, and suddenly the truth dawned on me that I had been made a fool of, and that everything had been prearranged between Mary and the Crown Prince.

I wondered desperately what would be the best thing for me to do. Should I wait on the chance of meeting Mary? should I go back to the carriage? or would it be wisest to go straight to the Baroness and tell her everything? As I stood pondering among the trees I suddenly saw a man looking at me fixedly, and terrified that I should be recognised, I waited no longer, but made my way back as quickly as possible to my carriage. The grand avenue was just in sight, when suddenly I came face to face with Rudolph and Mary. I started, for at the moment I did not recognise my cousin, who was wrapped in his long military cloak.

"Dear Marie," said he as he kissed my hand, "do forgive this little escapade, it is really of no consequence."

I was too angry to say a word, and I hurried on, followed by Mary. The Crown Prince apparently realised that silence was golden, and after saying good-bye in a rather shamefaced way, he left us.

As soon as the carriage was in motion, Mary looked out of the window, and then sank back with an exclamation of annoyance.

"How very annoying!" she observed.

"What is annoying? Your behaviour, I suppose," said I sharply.

"No, not exactly," she answered. "That hateful Herr von Pechy has been spying on us; I felt sure it was he, and now I'm certain."

I was horrified when I realised that the stranger I had seen in the wood might also have been Pechy, who was one of the worst gossips in existence. I turned to Mary. "Well, I hope you are satisfied now with the result of your plotting. Pechy will have spread the story all over Vienna by this time to-morrow, and my name will be dragged into it, for it certainly looks as if I had brought you here to keep a rendezvous with the Crown Prince. Mary, I'm amazed at your deceit."

"If I had told you, I don't think you would have taken me this afternoon," she replied, with disarming candour. "Oh, Marie, I *had* to see Rudolph somehow; fancy, Agnes has been ill for a week, and I've had nobody in whom I could confide. I managed to get a letter sent to him, and when I knew you were lunching with us I told him I would persuade you to go out with me afterwards."

"I'm very, very angry, " I said gravely; "you and Rudolph are utterly selfish; neither of you consider my position in the matter." Mary burst into tears, and between her sobs she assured me that she would not give me any more worry. It was really only a flirtation, nothing serious; she meant to give it up. "But please don't tell mamma." This was the drift of what she said:

"Mamma has no love for me," she continued. "Ever since I was a little girl she has treated me like something she means to dispose of to the best advantage. And Hannah, I - I detest her; she ought never to have left her convent, - her vocation is to be a nun, - then she and her tiresome painting wouldn't irritate me as they do now. I mean to marry, but you needn't grudge me a little happiness before I do. You know better than anyone what I shall have to expect from a *mariage de convenance*; just take your own case, you know you are miserable with Count Larisch."

I could not help feeling sorry for the excited girl.

"Look here, Mary, I will forgive you this once; we'll say no more about it - and you shall come with me to Jungenaum's. I'm going to have some gowns fitted."

The carriage stopped as I was speaking, and soon Mary appeared to have forgotten her troubles in the excitement of being shown the latest winter novelties. I was amazed to see how quickly her mood changed, but it was a good thing, I reflected, for when the time came for her to break with Rudolph, she would perhaps not feel the parting too much.

I took Mary to the Vetsera Palace, and returned to my hotel, where I found a telegram awaiting me. My youngest girl had met with an accident, and our doctor at Pardubitz wished for another opinion. I was dreadfully upset, and lost not a moment in sending for Professor Wiederhofer, who left Vienna with me the same evening.

The accident was not so serious as I was led to believe, but the illness and death of my grandfather, Duke Maximilien of Bavaria, which occurred soon afterwards, made it impossible for me to write to Mary as I had promised. However, it was not long before I received a letter from her, and I have rarely read such an hysterical effusion. Throughout it ran a vein of Oriental fatalism coupled with seething revolt against her destiny, and I could see how ardently she desired freedom and love. My heart ached for her, but I judged it best to refrain from sympathy when I answered her letter.

Early in December, Count Larisch and I went to Vienna for the Christmas shopping. The second day after our arrival George told me that he had accepted an invitation for us to dine at the Vetsera Palace. I stared at him in astonishment. "Whatever has changed your opinion of the Baroness?" I demanded.

"Oh, never mind," replied my husband. "I saw the Baroness to-day. Mary was with her; I'm quite surprised to see how pretty she has grown."

I smiled. So the naughty girl had evidently been trying to make a conquest of my husband!

That evening we dined with the Vetseras and met Mary's faithful admirer, the Duke of Braganza, who was related to me by his marriage with my cousin Elizabeth Taxis. Miguel was then a young and handsome widower, for Elizabeth had been dead for some years, and his two boys were under the care of the Archduchess Marie Therese. We had a delightful time, and I was quite sorry when George reminded me that we were due at the Opera.

"What! are you going to *Faust?*" cried Mary. "Do take me with you."

I glanced at my husband. I always disliked asking him for any favour, but I could not resist Mary's appeal. Luckily the Count had dined well, so my request was granted with unusual good-nature. I told Mary to get on her cloak, and when we entered her bedroom she kissed me with effusive gratitude.

"Oh, what a dear you are," she cried, and then busied herself at her toilet table. I saw that she was very excited, and when she arranged a magnificent diamond crescent in her dark hair, I could not help exclaiming, "But my child - we're not going to a ball." Agnes, who was in attendance, smiled maliciously, as much as to say: "How excessively simple you are," and Mary laughed.

"Why do you suppose I was anxious to go to the opera?" she asked. "To hear *Faust?* Not a bit of it. I want to go because the two Belgian peasants will be there, and I know how surprised they'll be to see me in your box."

"Now mind your behaviour," I insisted. "Please remember that I have no quarrel with the Crown Princess, and I think you display very questionable taste in flaunting yourself and your diamonds at the Opera this evening."

We hurried to our carriage, for it was already late; indeed, the first act was on when we arrived. I ensconced myself behind the velvet curtains, George was in the background, and Mary sat on my right in full view of the audience. She certainly looked radiantly beautiful. Her white crêpe-de-chine dress was the last word in costly simplicity, and her lovely neck and arms gleamed like ivory against the scarlet hangings of the box. Great diamond solitaires blazed. in her ears, and the crescent in her hair was a mass of prismatic colours. Her eyes sparkled, her cheeks were flushed, and her insolent gaze swept the Imperial box opposite, as she acknowledged Rudolph's presence with an impertinent little smile.

The Crown Princess and Louise of Coburg seemed highly amused when they saw Mary, and then with a refinement of maliciousness they both levelled their opera-glasses in her direction. I felt most uncomfortable, but fortunately Mary retained her self-possession, and the dreadful evening passed off better than I anticipated.

Early next morning my maid Jenny brought me a note, which she said required an answer. Jenny was a most trustworthy person, whose family had been for generations in the Imperial service, and she knew all the gossip of Vienna. When I asked who was waiting, she replied in a voice fraught with much meaning, "Mlle. Agnes."

The note was from Mary. Could I see her at five that afternoon? I considered for moment, and then wrote "Yes."

Mary was punctual. "Surely you are not angry," she said looking anxiously at me, for my manner was intentionally cold.

"I don't like the way you have of using me to suit your own purposes," I replied.

"But ... darling. I didn't do anything very shocking. Oh, did you ever see anything so ugly as those two Belgians? They've no figures, they are just like bundles of hay tied in the middle. I was sorry for Rudolph. Did you see how they stared at me?" asked Mary breathlessly.

"One thing at a time. Yes, I'll own the Princesses are not beautiful, but they can't help their looks, and it is no wonder they stared at you," I answered. "Oh, Mary, what a silly girl you are!"

"Well, they hate me, anyhow," she replied, "and Stéphanie calls me 'la petite.'"

"Who told you that?"

"Who else *could* know it but Rudolph?"

"Now, Mary," I said, "I feel convinced that you are keeping something back, and that you see and hear from Rudolph much more frequently than you tell me."

She blushed. "Oh, Marie, I'm sure I tell you all there is to tell; but - how long are you here for?"

"What do my movements matter to you?"

"Tell me, Marie - there's a dear."

"Well, for two or three days longer."

"Then It must be *to-morrow.*"

"I've had enough of your adventures," I told her; but she would not listen to me.

"You've simply got to come with me; I want to have a very special photograph taken at Adèle's."

"A present for the Crown Prince, I suppose?"

Mary made no reply, but before she took leave of me I had weakly consented to do as she wished, and we duly went to Adèle's.

"I'll give you the best," she told me, when the sitting was over, and then an idea seized her. "Why, Marie, darling - let's be photographed together; we may never get the chance again. Come along." And she almost dragged me into the studio.

Later I had every reason to regret that this fatal photograph was ever taken. But the future was then mercifully hidden from me.

We spent Christmas at Pardubitz. It was bitter weather; deep snow covered the ground, and during the long dull evenings my thoughts reverted to the South. I had an intense longing for the blue skies of the Riviera; I desired sun and warmth, and I shivered as I looked out over the wintry landscape. No news came from Vienna although I had received Mary's photograph on Christmas morning. Underneath it were the enigmatic words, "Treu bis in den Tod" (True till Death). "This is the last photograph I shall ever have done," she wrote. "I intend to imitate the Empress, and never allow anyone to remember me except as a pretty young girl."

Poor child, she little dreamed how tragically her words were soon to come true.

I was vaguely uneasy, but I put down my unusual nervousness to my depressing surroundings. George was fidgeting about his health, and told me, to my great joy, that he had made up his mind to leave for the Riviera almost at once, and not to wait until our usual February exodus. He always imagined he was hovering on the brink of the grave, and the slightest cough or cold was sufficient to alarm him.

"Well, if you are really going South, I must go to Vienna and get some clothes," I told him.

"By all means," he assented; "take Jenny and go a few days in advance; but - I may as well tell you - I've lost the good opinion I was beginning to have of Mary Vetsera. The girl is a cocotte at heart, and I won't have you too friendly with her."

"Why, what has Mary done now?"

He smiled, and looked things unutterable.

"Tell me, I'm really curious," I said.

"Do you remember that day you went with her to Adèle's? Well, she actually had the impudence to say, 'I'm going to be photographed especially for *you*, dear Count, because I know how much you love me.'"

"Did you believe she meant what she said?"

"Marie, that girl meant to lure me on to make her a declaration," affirmed my husband gravely. "Of course, I can't help attracting women - but I don't encourage them."

"Oh, George! how dense you are," was my rejoinder.

CHAPTER XI
I GIVE MY AID

An unexpected visitor - The Crown Prince - What Rudolph had to say - The woman in the case - The weariness of life - Rudolph tells me his plans for Mary's future - I review the situation - Am I a pawn in his game? - "Beware of Rudolph" - I see Mary - Her changed appearance - I hear her laugh for the last time - I go to the Vetsera Palace - Dressing for the ball - Mary's beauty - An outburst - Drive to the German Embassy - What happened there - Mary insults the Crown Princess - A social downfall

I telegraphed to secure our usual rooms at the Grand Hotel, and came to Vienna with Jenny in attendance. As by chance I travelled part of the way from Pardubitz with a gossiping friend of the Vetseras, I felt sure that the Baroness would in consequence soon hear of my arrival in the Capital. But to my great surprise I heard nothing from Mary, and could not help wondering if anything unexpected had happened since last we met.

After five o'clock in the afternoon, two days after I had arrived, I returned from doing some shopping, and, having taken off my hat and coat, I was just going to ring for Jenny, when, to my surprise, she hurriedly entered the salon. The maid, who looked flustered, said to me in an agitated whisper, "The Crown Prince is here," and the words were hardly out of her mouth when a tall figure, dressed in a military cloak, walked into my room. It was my cousin.

Rudolph had turned up the collar of his cloak; he wore his kepi well down over his eyes, and for some moments I stared at him in astonishment. Then he stepped forward and kissed my hand, saying as he did so, "I hope you'll forgive this informal call, Marie." I was silent, and my cousin looked at me with his mocking smile.

"Have you then forgotten mamma's lessons on the necessity of self-control? You look like a startled schoolgirl."

"I never expected to have the honour of a visit from you," I said.

"Well, my dear cousin, it's absolutely necessary that I should see you." He sat down as he spoke, but did not remove his cloak. "Now - I will be brief and tell you the reason of my coming here. You know all about the little Vetsera girl and myself."

"I know something," I replied, at once on my guard.

"An answer worthy of your education at Gödöllő. You can't deceive me, Marie, you know all."

"Well, perhaps I do, but I am not too sure."

"I hope you don't imagine that this is a platonic friendship?" said the Prince, "because if you do I had better disillusion you at once. The affair is not at all innocent; in fact I'm in the devil of a mess in more ways than one. I rely upon you to help me."

"How did you know that I was in Vienna?" I asked.

"Through Mary, of course, although I haven't spoken to her for days. Anyhow, we correspond and she sends her letters to me by Agnes. There is some gossip about us which has reached the old lady's ears" (this was how my cousin always designated the Baroness), "and the poor child is spied on and scolded until she is nearly desperate."

"I suppose Herr von Pechy has started the scandal?"

"Precisely - and you know what he is."

I nodded. "He's dangerous; but, Rudolph, however could you be so foolish as to get into this entanglement?"

The Crown Prince shrugged his shoulders. "Nothing is so easy for a man as to become entangled with a pretty woman, and Mary is, a perfect little devil. The bother is that she has lost her head, and unless you do something to steady her, she will kick over the traces and cause a regular scandal. I don't want that."

"No," I assented; "but you have shaken off many feminine encumbrances in your time. Why not Mary?"

"Simply because she won't be shaken off, I tell you," said Rudolph crossly. "Goodness knows I have tried my utmost to persuade her to accept Miguel Braganza; it would suit me admirably, for I believe I have a positive genius for playing the rôle of the family friend."

"You were to blame in the first instance, Rudolph; you were horribly selfish to disturb Mary's peace of mind, and now that you've made your bed, I am very much afraid you will have to lie on it. I can't help you. Besides," I added, "why do you come to me? We have never professed any particular friendship for each other; in fact, deep down, I don't like you any more than you like me. Let us be frank, and acknowledge this."

The Crown Prince had risen from his seat, and was standing by the window, drumming the panes with nervous fingers. Suddenly he came over to me, and took my hand, and something in his unhappy face recalled the memory of the day when I had seen his mother weep under the tree at Garatshausen. I let my hand rest in his, and I thought that perhaps after all I had no right to refuse him my assistance. He was of my blood, my own cousin, and the son of my beloved aunt, whom I had always obeyed so blindly. "Rudolph, I will help you," I said.

"I was certain I could trust you," he replied. "Listen: this intrigue would not matter so much if it did not clash with far more important things. I cannot waste my time on love, because there are urgent matters which I dare not disregard. You know how badly Stéphanie and I get on; you know that my father is unsympathetic, and I need not remind you how little my mother loves me. Altogether, I'm in a bad way ..."

Rudolph released my hand and walked up and down the room, every movement betraying his agitation. "Oh, I'm tired of life! I only wish I had the courage and independence of John of Tuscany; he is a free spirit anyhow, who has escaped the mire of Court intrigue. You know the baseness of it all; you have been behind the scenes, and you know what despicable puppets we are. We are dressed up to please the people; we dance to the tune of others; we dare not be natural. O my God, why was I born? At the best what am I? A poor creature cursed with the sins of my progenitors."

I was alarmed at this outburst and endeavoured to soothe him, but he took no notice of me.

"Still," he continued, "perhaps I am unwise to despise this poor little girl's affection. She does not aspire to play the Pompadour; my rank matters little to her. She is just a woman who loves me. I've known many far more beautiful, but I have never met with a more faithful heart."

"Rudolph, don't distress yourself so much," I entreated.

"I'm not absolutely devoid of feeling," he replied, "and my better self urges me to try and save Mary before it is too late. We must not meet until my affairs are more settled. You and Larisch are going to the Riviera. Can't you persuade the Baroness and Mary to accompany you - anything to get the child away from Vienna? Tell her I'll join her incognito; promise anything you like, but help me now."

"I'm afraid it will be difficult to arrange a marriage for Mary," I said. "The Vetseras are rich, and Mary is not obliged to marry the first man who proposes for her."

"The Vetseras *rich?*" queried Rudolph in real astonishment. "Why, don't you know that the Baroness is living on her capital, which is nearly exhausted? Mary represents the last throw of the dice."

I was dumbfounded, but did not doubt that my cousin was speaking the truth. However, I had no time to continue the conversation, for I had promised to dine with my sister-in-law, and it was already getting late. Rudolph noticed that I showed signs of restlessness. "I am sure I am detaining you," he remarked. "But do tell Mary what I suggest she should do."

"Now, Rudolph," I said, "once my word is given it is given. I will do my best in this unpleasant business, and will see Mary to-morrow."

"Oh, Marie, you will really do this for me?"

"I have said I will."

"Then write me the result of the interview. You can send me a letter to my apartments in the Burg. I'm alone there with Loschek, and be sure that your letter is only given into his hands. Good-bye, dear cousin, you have no idea what a load you have taken off my mind."

I reflected rather ruefully that he had shifted his burden upon my unwilling shoulders, but as I had promised to help him I felt I must stand by my word.

"Did anyone recognise you when you came here this afternoon?" I asked.

"No," he answered, "I came up unnoticed by the servants' staircase, and Bratfisch is waiting for me with his fiacre outside the cabmen's restaurant in the Maxmilienstrasse."

"Oh, Bratfisch can be trusted," I said, quite reassured, for that good-natured man would have laid down his life for my cousin. He knew all about the Crown Prince's intrigues, and I firmly believe that if Rudolph had told him to drive to Hell, Bratfisch would have endeavoured to find the nearest way there.

Jenny later corroborated my cousin's statement. She had met him in the corridor, and he had asked to be shown into my rooms at once. "Will your Imperial Highness wait a moment until I announce you?" asked the maid; but Rudolph had followed close on her heels.

We were both thoroughly unsettled by the events of the afternoon. Jenny knew that something unexpected must have brought the Crown Prince to see me, and I could plainly see that she thought Mary Vetsera was at the bottom of it.

I was greatly depressed during dinner, and everybody noticed my loss of spirits. I was heartily glad to return to my hotel, but my sleep was disturbed, and I dreamt horrible dreams in which I figured with Rudolph and Mary in desperate adventures. I awoke un refreshed, and my usually placid temper suffered in consequence. I could not shake off a feeling of uneasiness. I wondered whether Rudolph was merely using me as a pawn, and I remembered that my distrust of him dated back to the days. of my childhood. I was accustomed to be made use of by my various relations, but their intrigues were generally romantic and harmless, and, better still, soon over and as soon forgotten. But the Prince was not like my amorous family, and I had hitherto not played with fire.

I recalled Elizabeth's words, "Beware of Rudolph." The Empress no doubt had some good reason for warning me against her son. He was not to be trusted, she had said, and he could be a dangerous enemy. Why had I allowed myself to be carried away by a sudden impulse and to promise my help? It was quite possible that Mary and Rudolph were playing some deep game. Were they? I wondered. Then I decided that I would not waste another minute, so I went to my writing-table and began to write a letter to Mary.

I was spared doing so, however, for Jenny announced the Baroness Mary Vetsera and her *promeneuse*, a lady whose duty it was to accompany her whenever she went out.

I advanced and kissed Mary, who turned to her companion and said, "Do you mind waiting for me in Jenny's room? I want to speak to Countess Larisch alone."

The *promeneuse* went out with Jenny, and Mary threw herself into an armchair and lit a cigarette. She was very nervous and excited, and my attention was arrested by the marked change in her appearance, for her blue eyes had a look of that knowledge which can only be imparted by constant intercourse with a lover. Mary looked different. Her red mouth was set in a hard line, and she clicked her high heels together with an impatient movement.

"Well, Marie," she commenced, with just a slight touch of insolence in her voice, "you see I'm here in person to listen to your sermon."

"My dear girl ... "I remonstrated; but she continued, as if repeating a well-learned lesson:

"He wrote and told me to come. I know he was here yesterday. I'm to be good and talk sensibly. It's all *here* ..." She tapped her bodice, and I could hear the crackle of paper as she did so. "I'm *quite* ready to listen."

"Mary, Mary, why are you so discourteous? I thought you looked upon me as your, friend."

Her mood changed; her face softened; sudden tears drowned the hateful knowledge in her eyes, and she threw her arms around me, sobbing bitterly.

"Oh, Marie darling, do get me away from Vienna. I shall die if I have to remain at home. You've no idea what a cruel mother I have! Mamma wants to sell me. I'm the only thing that can save us all from ruin. Oh, dear, what a miserable girl I am. ..."

"Hannah will never marry well," continued Mary. "I know I'm considered pretty, and I suppose I must do as I am told when the time comes. I love Rudolph, but I will not become a worry to him. He wants me to go away from Vienna. Must I?"

"Dearest child, he only thinks a change to the Riviera would benefit you," I said.

Mary smiled through her tears. "I know what *that* means. Oh, I'm not the stupid little girl of a month ago, I'm much more sensible now. Rudolph has told me about his troubles, and a good deal about the dreadful situation in which he finds himself. I am better away from Vienna, but I'm afraid to leave him alone just now when he requires so much support."

I stared, for I was surprised to see how womanly Mary had become.

"Tell me all he said, "she pleaded. I told her, and as she seemed rather disappointed I felt certain she had reason to believe that by rights I ought to know something more, but she did not enlighten me.

"I must go now," exclaimed Mary. "Oh, I know, there was another thing I wanted to say. We are going to a ball to-night at the German Embassy. I've the loveliest gown. Do come and see me dressed."

"I can't impose myself on your mother without an invitation, so late in the evening," I reminded her.

"Never mind mamma," she retorted, "she's only too glad to see the niece of the Empress whenever she chooses to come."

"Very well. I'll be delighted. And Mary, *be good.*"

She laughed her pretty laugh, and it was the last time I ever heard it.

I sat down and wrote to Rudolph. "It is quite all right," I told him, "my mission is over. Mary is amenable to reason, and makes no objection to leaving Vienna." I asked Jenny to deliver my note at the Burg, and felt a great deal easier in my mind after I had written it.

I reached the Vetsera Palace that night about eight o'clock, and as I did not think I should remain long I instructed my coachman to wait. When I arrived the Baroness and her daughters were taking tea in the smoking-room; both girls wore dressing-gowns, and the curl on Mary's forehead was still *en papillote*. She was flushed and excited, in striking contrast to Hannah's quiet, satirical mood, while the Baroness Vetsera seemed in great spirits.

"I wonder how you'll like Mary's gown," asked Hannah, helping herself to a caviare sandwich; it's from the Maison Spitzer; mamma thinks it lovely. Oh, Mary," she added, looking across at her sister, "for the love of heaven, don't take so much rum in your tea; eat something instead." Her sister made no reply, but lit a cigarette, which annoyed her mother. "How often must I remind you never to smoke before you go to a ball?" observed the Baroness, fretfully; "really you are past praying for."

Mary got up and went out, and as she banged the door behind her, Hannah remarked: "Now you see what we have to put up with from Mary; it's all your fault, mamma; if you were to be firm for once, you would have no further trouble."

I followed Mary to her room, and found her seated before her toilette table. Her hands played nervously with the pretty trifles of silver and crystal, but her thoughts seemed far away, and at first I do not think she noticed me.

Agnes put on the fine silk stockings and satin shoes, and I looked round the pretty bedroom, which was an ideal sanctum for a young girl. A picture of the Madonna hung over the little white bed; photographs stood on the mantelpiece and on the writing-table, and the windows were covered with bead blinds. Mary had a habit of standing and pulling off the beads whenever she was nervous or worried. I noticed many bare strings that night.

I sat down to watch Agnes dress Mary's beautiful brown hair, and then fix the glittering diamond crescent high in the artistically arranged coils. The young girl was still wrapped in her own thoughts, and I could not help thinking how perfectly lovely she looked, although dark thoughts seemed to hold her in their thrall.

"Will the 'Princess' graciously allow Agnes to come and help me for a moment ?" asked Hannah, putting her head in at the door.

Mary told her maid she did not require her; she then busied herself with polishing her nails, and afterwards she put on her many beautiful rings. Then she turned to me.

"Do I look nice?" she asked, anxiously.

I smiled. Did she look nice? I had never seen a fairer picture, and I had no hesitation in telling her so.

"Do you think I shall be admired?"

"I'm positive you will."

She smiled coldly. "Oh, then *she* will be jealous."

"And pray who is she?" I said.

"Why, Rudolph's stupid, stuck-up Belgian wife."

"Mary, you must not say such things; I don't like to hear them; they are not true."

Her eyes looked positively evil. "Never mind, you'd hate her if you knew all I do. She makes Rudolph's life miserable; she won't understand him, and instead of being a help to him she drags him down. Stéphanie's nothing but a fool. Oh, Marie, Rudolph is so unfortunate; every one is against him and I wish I could always be with him. *But if trouble comes, I shall never forsake him.*"

She said these last words in a hurried undertone, and Agnes came to tell us that the carriage was waiting.

Mary wore a light-blue dress trimmed with yellow, one of Spitzer's exquisite creations; a true-lover's knot of diamonds blazed in her corsage, and I could not help thinking that both she and her mother wore too many diamonds.

Madame Vetsera was in black velvet, with a necklace of diamond ivy leaves, and diamond pins fastened the white aigrette in her hair. Hannah was simply dressed in white, and a row of pearls was her only ornament.

I was just going to say good-bye, when Mary exclaimed:

"Do me a favour if you love me, Marie."

"What is it?" I asked.

"Let me drive to the Embassy with *you*; it isn't far, and mamma and Hannah will have much more room without me."

I assented. Agnes came forward with the fur-trimmed evening wraps, and we went downstairs together.

Mary put her arm around my waist directly we were alone. "Oh, what a relief it is not to be shut up with mamma in the other carriage; she would lecture me the whole time." And she trembled as she spoke.

"What has agitated you, dear child?" I asked. "I could see you were quite *bouleversée* this evening."

"Oh, Marie, he has written to me, something troubles him; he wants to see me. How I wish he would throw everything to the winds and come away with us to the Riviera. ..." But by this time we had reached the Embassy, and Mary, after kissing me good-night, joined her mother and sister.

Afterwards I heard all about Mary's behaviour, which scandalised society that disastrous evening. The ball was a brilliant spectacle, and the Imperial family were present when the Vetseras arrived. Mary was the cynosure of all eyes, chiefly on account of her beauty, but also because the seeds sown by Herr von Pechy's gossip were beginning to bear fruit. Rudolph's name was coupled with hers, and several well-known women eyed Mary with disapproving glances. This treatment stung the already overwrought girl into madness, and when the Imperial guests moved about the ballroom and spoke to their various acquaintances, Mary was burning to take her revenge. She smiled when Rudolph exchanged a few words with her, but as the Crown Princess passed she looked Stéphanie full in the face and did not acknowledge her presence. The eyes of the two women met, and I am told that they looked for all the world like tigers ready to spring.

The onlookers were stupefied, and just as everybody wondered what would happen next, Mary stamped her foot once - twice - and then flung her head back with a movement of supreme contempt.

The Baroness Vetsera, who had watched the scene in terror, now came up, crimson with anger and shame at her daughter's public affront to the Crown Princess. She seized Mary by the arm, and made a hurried exit from the ballroom. Her departure loosened the flood-gates of conversation, and soon nearly all those present who had enjoyed Madame Vetsera's hospitality were rejoicing like "good Christians" in the prospect of her daughter's social downfall.

CHAPTER XII
A TRUST IMPOSED

A disturbing letter - What does the Crown Prince want with me? - I resolve not to see him - In the toils - "I want you to bring Mary to the Hofburg" - Rudolph tells me his difficulties - The Steel Box - R. I. U. O. - "My own death warrant" - No chance of escape - A visitor - Mary Vetsera - Why she came - Her mother's anger - The iron bangle - "I shall drown myself" - I take Mary home - The Baroness is relieved - The last night - "Their love, and their hatred, and their envy is now perished" - I interview Madame Vetsera - She discloses her hand - A delicate mission

I heard nothing about the ball from Mary.

The following day I was very busy, and at bed-time was so tired that I told Jenny not to awaken me early. I was therefore rather annoyed when she came into my room a little before eight o'clock. I was very drowsy, but soon became wide awake, when I grasped the fact that Bratfisch had brought a note from the Crown Prince. It consisted of a few lines only.

"I must speak to you alone," wrote Rudolph. "Wait in at five this afternoon; be sure you are alone, and let Jenny see that the coast is clear on the servants' staircase."

This communication made me horribly nervous, and I was also very angry, because I felt keenly Rudolph's lack of consideration about the false position in which his behaviour was bound to place me. I made up my mind to have nothing more to do with him and his affairs, as I knew that if the Empress ever heard of the part I had played, she would never forgive me.

When I reviewed the events of the past few days, I was more than ever surprised at Rudolph's attitude. I remembered the days at Gödöllõ when he had made sneering remarks about my position there, and had designated me "the Confidential Mistress of the Horse to the Empress." On another occasion he had called me "a talebearer," and had laughed at our simple life at Munich. I also felt that he disliked me on account of the affection which his mother had for me. At last I worked myself up into a regular state of nerves. I jumped out of bed, and wrote a note to my cousin saying that I absolutely refused to see him.

I rang for my maid. "Get on your things at once," I said, "and take this letter to the Burg. Ask to see Loschek, and be sure you give it to nobody but him."

I was nearly dressed by the time she returned and words cannot express my feelings when she handed me my own letter, and told me that the Crown Prince had left Vienna for Laxenburg. This unexpected setback to my plans greatly disturbed me. Jenny was positive that my cousin was away, as his private apartments were being "turned out" when she arrived.

There seemed no escape for me. I felt that it was useless to make any further attempts to avoid the interview and I resigned myself to my fate. It was a dark, foggy day, and the hours passed with leaden feet, but punctually at five o'clock Rudolph made his appearance. As on the occasion of his first visit, the Prince was wrapped in his military cloak, but this time he did not greet me. He was very excited, and his first words were:

"Marie - if you don't help me *everything* is lost."

I gazed at him without speaking. My cousin was a changed man; he looked pale and worn, and his eyes gleamed with that curious wolfish light which I had always noticed when he was excited. I felt instinctively that something dreadful had happened; some sort of hypnotic feeling overcame me, and I felt I could not resist doing whatever he wished.

We were both standing, and I could hear Rudolph's hurried breathing, which, except for the ticking of the clock, alone broke the tense stillness of the room.

"For heaven's sake," I stammered, "tell me what is wrong."

"Oh, you cannot possibly realise the trouble in which I am plunged," replied Rudolph, "but before I go into my own worries, I had better tell you that Mary is locked up in her room."

"Locked up - why?" I ejaculated.

"She and the 'old lady' had a terrible scene after the ball," said the Crown Prince. "That hateful Taxis woman, who lives opposite the Vetsera Palace, has apparently seen Mary going out at night, and promptly chose the worst time to tell the Baroness." He smiled drily. "It was not to be supposed that she was over pleased at Mary's behaviour to Stéphanie; you know all about it, I suppose?"

I nodded. "Yes; and then?"

"Then Mary was locked up. And only you can get her out."

"Rudolph, I will not interfere."

"I say that you *will*. I must speak to her."

"You are mad."

"No, no, I'm sane enough. Listen. I want you *to bring Mary to me at the* Hofburg."

I grasped the back of a chair to steady myself, for I was staggered at his suggestion, and repeated his words mechanically.

"Bring Mary to the Hofburg!"

"Yes, I insist. Listen, Marie; nothing will be easier. You must persuade the Baroness to allow Mary to go out with you, and then you must drive to the private entrance, and Loschek will bring you direct to my rooms."

"I can't ... I won't. *I won't do it.*" And then a wave of furious anger swept over me. "How dare you try to ruin me!" I panted. "I hate you ... get out of my sight." Then I collapsed on the couch and began to cry quietly.

Rudolph bent over me. "Marie, dear," he said, in his fascinating tone of persuasion, "don't make a scene, for if anyone hears, there'll be such a scandal. I assure you it is necessary for me to see Mary. Besides, I myself am in great danger."

I raised my head. "*You* in danger?"

"Yes, in very great danger. We are now speaking 'man to man.' You are the only person in whom I can place absolute confidence. Swear to me that while I live you will never disclose what I am going to tell you."

"If I can avert the danger, I will. I swear it, Rudolph."

The Crown Prince looked at me very strangely. Then, without a word, he took a small dark object from under his cloak. I could see that it was a box sewn up in cloth. I shrank back unconsciously, but my cousin put his disengaged hand on my shoulder. "Listen, Marie; you must take this box and put it away in a safe place at once. It is imperative that it should not be found in my possession, for at any moment the Emperor may order my personal belongings to be seized."

"The Emperor?" I gasped.

"Yes, the Emperor." With that the Crown Prince handed me the box, and when I took it I was astonished to find that it was nearly as heavy as lead. "It is a steel casket," observed Rudolph, who noticed my surprise.

"But I can't take it with me when I am travelling," I objected.

"You must put the box in your trunk; it will be easily hidden there, and nothing inside it can possibly compromise you."

"How long am I to keep this dreadful thing in my possession?"

"Until I ask for it," answered Rudolph, "or until some one else asks for it. If it should come to that," he added, gravely, "you must know how to act. There is one person who knows the secret of this casket, and he alone has the right (failing me) to ask for its return."

"His name?"

"Never mind his name. You can deliver it to the person who can tell you four letters. Write them down now, and repeat them after me. Listen," and the Crown Prince slowly uttered the letters: "R.I.U.O."

I repeated them, and wrote them down in a little pocket-book. Then, as if controlled by some stronger will than my own, I took the mysterious box into my bedroom and hid it at the bottom of my large travelling trunk. I also wrote R.I.U.O. on a corner of the lining, and then turned the key in the lock.

"I do not like this business," I said dubiously when I again sat down beside my cousin.

Rudolph tried to reassure me. "It's not so very terrible," he answered. "But now, Marie, time passes, and I must arrange about your visit to the Hofburg to-morrow."

"Oh, it's madness; it's madness," I repeated. "I can't do it."

"Be quiet; I know you will do it. I must speak to Mary *alone*; it may possibly help me to escape the trouble which threatens me."

I did not quite believe this latter statement, but I asked: "Does the trouble concern your dissensions with Stéphanie?"

Rudolph laughed. "Stéphanie! - Oh dear me, no; she's merely a domestic trouble. The danger which menaces me is political!"

I was now thoroughly alarmed, for I never suspected that the Crown Prince would be so mad as to embroil himself in dangerous political intrigues.

"Oh," I said. "I implore you, Rudolph, lose no time. Confide in the Empress, or ... better still, go to the Emperor."

"You fool," he exclaimed; - then more gently, "I don't mean that, Marie. Listen. If I were to confide in the Emperor, *I should sign my own Death Warrant*." My heart nearly stopped beating at this dreadful disclosure, and I could say nothing. "Now about Mary," he continued. "You must pretend that you want to take her shopping; get a fiacre and tell the man to drive you behind the palace of the Archduke Albert, which joins on to part of the walls of the Hofburg. You will notice a small iron door; go up to it and Loschek will be awaiting your arrival. It has been a very useful door," said Rudolph, "and many of my charming friends have preferred to come to Court that way."

"Will you promise me that you will not play me false if I bring Mary?"

"I promise you that I will not involve you in any scandal," was the reply.

"Very well," said I; "you might also remember that I have to return to Pardubitz very shortly, so say all you have to say at this next meeting."

"Oh, trust me to do that," answered Rudolph, "and I will never forget what you have done for me ... so now farewell, until to-morrow."

Left alone, I felt faint with terror, but I grew calmer when I thought that after all I should soon be away from Vienna, and I decided that I would see as little as possible of Mary on the Riviera. But, as I had given my word to Rudolph, I wrote to the Baroness Vetsera, and asked whether she would allow Mary to go out with me the next day. If so, I would call for her some time during the morning.

Jenny took the note, and brought back the answer; it was in the affirmative. I hesitated no longer - I felt it was useless. I had tried to escape from Rudolph, I had given the Baroness a chance to refuse my request; but Fate was too strong for me.

That evening my pleasant acquaintance, Madame Muller, a dear old lady who occasionally executed my commissions, supped with me. She was a typical Viennese, and a most entertaining woman; so I was very glad to see her, and temporarily to forget my troubles.

"Every one is speaking about the Crown Prince and Mary Vetsera," Madame Muller informed me. "But, there ... it's only another of his many flirtations. At any rate, the little Baroness is far safer than that intriguing Princess P- for 'unser Rudi.' The Vetseras don't count for much," she went on. "The mother knows all about it, I am told, and shuts her eyes; but the affair is not very serious."

Our conversation was interrupted by a timid knock. "Come in," I said, somewhat impatiently. The door opened, and a heavily veiled lady entered the room. Madame Muller and I looked at her in astonishment. Then all at once I realised who it was. "*Mary!*" I cried.

Mary Vetsera stared at me with a sort of terrible composure. I made a sign to Madame Muller to go into Jenny's room, and then Mary slowly took off the veil which covered her head. She was deathly pale, and her eyes seemed far too big for her face; she looked as if something dreadful had happened to her.

I was now thoroughly alarmed, and took her in my arms. "Mary dear, speak to me," I begged.

She commenced to tremble violently. "For God's sake tell me what has happened," I cried.

Mary sank into a chair with a movement of excessive weariness. I unfastened her sealskin coat, and then noticed that she was wearing a thin house frock and slippers.

"Oh ... Oh, don't send me back," she exclaimed feverishly. "Marie, I've run away. If you won't shelter me I'll throw myself in the Danube. I can't live at home any longer. Lock the door, I may be followed ... " - her voice rose almost to a shriek. "I won't be taken away."

"Darling, be calm," I urged; "tell me what has happened. I won't send you away."

Mary broke into shuddering sobs. "Ever since the ball ... Mamma ... dreadful. She struck me in the carriage. ... She and Hannah were like furies. I can't remember all the horrid things they said. When I reached home I threw myself on my bed ... I must have fainted."

"Poor child!" I murmured.

"When I came to myself I discovered that I was a prisoner. It was morning; Hannah brought me my coffee, but she said that I was not to stir out of my room. The hours passed. I was nearly mad. I imagined all sorts of things and then I made up my mind to send a letter to Rudolph. I managed to write a note in pencil which I gave to Agnes, and I waited anxiously for the interview which I felt I must have eventually with mamma.

"How interminable the time seemed, and how miserable I felt! Marie, I wonder whether I am always to be unhappy; sometimes I think that my love for Rudolph is fatal; yet it's strong, it holds me, and I would rather suffer through it than live without it."

Mary looked at me sadly, and then with a sudden change of mood said in tones of bitter contempt:

"I had to wait until this evening before I saw mamma. She came to my room, and told me that she had fully made up her mind to send me into a 'retreat' until I came to my senses. But when I made no reply she lost her temper and told me – what *do* you think?"

"I have no idea."

"Mamma blamed *me* for bringing disgrace on our family - the virtuous Vetseras!" said Mary with a hard expression on her face. "But I was silent, Marie, all her taunts and reproaches were useless."

"What happened after that?" I asked.

"Mamma noticed the iron ring and the iron bangle which I always wear, and said angrily, 'I believe the Crown Prince gave you these stupid things, but anyhow I shall know the truth about them from Countess Larisch.'"

"Why was *my* name brought into it?" I asked, much surprised.

"Oh, Marie, darling," cried Mary apologetically, "I never told you. Rudolph did give me the ring and the bangle, but I was obliged to tell mamma that they were a present from you."

I was not over-pleased to hear of her deceit, especially as she had not taken me into her confidence, and I might have innocently betrayed her. "I never saw them," I remarked.

"I wear so many bangles and rings," answered Mary, "but look *now* - " and as she spoke she stretched out her left hand. There was a thin iron ring on the fourth finger, and on her arm was a thin iron bangle.

"What an odd notion," I said. "I don't I think iron jewellery is particularly pretty; what is the meaning of it?"

"Rudolph wears the same," Mary replied. "He says it signifies 'True till Death.'"

I could not help thinking that it would be a good thing for everyone if Mary were sent into temporary seclusion; but the next moment I hated the selfish thought, when I saw how ill and unhappy the poor child seemed. One thing was certain; she must return home that night.

"How did you manage to get away, Mary?"

"Mamma went out in a rage, and I heard her talking to Hannah in the smoking-room. Then Agnes came. I implored her to help me; I offered her money - anything. She promised to assist me; I slipped on my coat, and ran downstairs unobserved; once out of the house I hailed a fiacre and came to you."

"Darling, let me take you back; your mother will forgive you if I ask her. Mary, be reasonable."

"If *you* cast me off, I shall drown myself," she said.

I felt worried to death. I pointed out that the Baroness would surely guess she had come to me, and some one might be expected at any moment.

Mary flung her arms around me. "Dear Marie!" she sobbed, "I know I'm selfishly dragging you into my miserable affairs, but I *do* love you."

The poor girl was nearly in hysterics, and I could not reason with her. At last I inquired: "Did your mother mention my letter?"

"No; what letter?"

I told Mary about the arrangement between Rudolph and myself. "Now," I said, "won't the prospect of seeing him to-morrow make you go home quietly?"

Her April mood was upon her; she uttered a little cry of joy, and smiles succeeded her tears. Yes she would return, but only if I would accompany her. And then to see Rudolph again, that would be heaven.

"Very well, let us go at once," I said. "Now Mary, promise me to keep your temper if your mother is very angry, and I'll do my best to dissuade her from the idea of sending you to a convent. Now, are you ready to start?"

Mary shivered visibly, but rapidly gained her self-control. I rang for Jenny and told her to send for a fiacre; then I made a hurried toilet, and we went downstairs together.

Mary had another *crise des nerfs* when she saw the fiacre, and I breathed more freely when we were safely inside; but when we approached the Salesianergasse she became dreadfully agitated, and I thought she would jump out of the vehicle.

"Oh, Marie, don't, don't leave me alone with mamma," she begged.

"Dear child, rely on me," I said; "I promise you that I will do my best for you." The fiacre stopped as I spoke. We alighted, and I told the man to wait.

The Vetsera Palace was almost in darkness, and the concierge did not answer my ring. After waiting a few minutes the door was opened by Agnes, who exclaimed when she saw me: "Countess, for pity's sake is the Baroness Mary with you?"

I told her yes, and as we reached the top of the staircase we encountered Hannah, who looked scared to death.

"Oh, *have* you brought Mary?" she cried.

"Yes," I said, trying to speak lightly, "this impulsive young lady came to see me quite unexpectedly."

"Oh, I'm so glad, for mamma is nearly dead, and the servants are looking for Mary everywhere."

I went first into the boudoir. At all times the Baroness liked a subdued light, but now only one lamp was lit, and I could just make out a huddled-up figure on the sofa. I felt terribly ill at ease while Hannah went over to her mother. "Don't fret any longer, mamma," said she, "that naughty girl only went as far as the Grand Hotel after all, and Countess Larisch has brought her safely home."

The Baroness raised herself, and gave me her hand. Then she looked indignantly at Mary but said nothing.

"Don't be angry, Hélène," I pleaded, "the child is quite worn out; to-morrow you can talk things over. Mary doesn't mean to make you unhappy."

"She had better go to bed," said the Baroness. She kissed her daughter in silence, and Hannah whispered, "Tell mamma how sorry you are, Mary. "Her sister took no notice, but turned to me.

"Do come and see me into bed, Marie, I shall sleep better if you do."

I followed her into the pretty bedroom. Hannah came with us, and quietly helped Mary to undress; then she went away and we were alone.

"Promise me you will really come to-morrow," she said.

"I promise. And you will promise to be my own dear little friend and not to give us any more pain. Your mother really loves you, and perhaps everything in your life will change for the better. Be brave, Mary: you are so young, and there are many happy days in store for you yet."

I kissed her tenderly, and thought how lovely she looked as she lay back on her pillows. I often think of Mary as I saw her that night - the last she was destined to spend under her mother's roof. She was to know a bitter-sweet hour of love, to drink the wine of passion, and to pass tragically from those on earth. For Mary Vetsera and Another were soon to be numbered with those who "know not anything."

"Also their love, and their hatred, and their envy, is now perished; neither have they any more a portion ... in anything that is done under the sun."

I closed the bedroom door gently. Hannah was waiting in the passage. "Mamma would like to talk to you," she said, "do go in for a moment. Now you can see for yourself what Mary is, as the result of mamma's education. It is high time something was done, and the sooner she is sent away the better."

I went to the boudoir, and found the Baroness, who seemed greatly relieved to see me.

"I feel sure I can speak freely to you, dear Marie," she said, "because I am sure that you know *all*."

"I do not know what you mean by all," I answered.

"Oh, dear, I allude to Mary's affair with the Crown Prince. I'm convinced she is *liée* with him, but I do hope nothing serious has happened between them."

"I know nothing about the extent of their intimacy."

"Of course he is very unhappy," continued the Baroness, "and there are rumours that he wishes to divorce Stéphanie. I don't want my daughter to be openly compromised, although there are many who would jump at the prospect of a liaison with the Crown Prince. You are his cousin; will you undertake a very delicate mission for me? I want you to talk plainly to the Prince about Mary. You might even give him a hint that matters might be arranged if he is really desperately in love with her. I only wish we lived in the times of Louis XV," said the perplexed lady. "Favourites like Madame de Pompadour and the Dubarry were then quite recognised by society. How explained away! I sometimes think," she added, "that my father was quite right when he said that the Sultan of Turkey got the best out of life so far as women were concerned."

She sighed - perhaps at the thought of what Mary had missed through being born a century or so too late. "At any rate, I've no objection to discussing the subject with the Crown Prince. Do you think you could see him and tell him so? If he once realises that I know all about this flirtation, he will feel much more at ease with me."

"Oh, very well," I answered. "I'll try and have an interview with Rudolph before I leave Vienna. By-the-bye, I shall fetch Mary at eleven o'clock to-morrow morning. Good-night, Hélène, and don't be angry with Mary. Believe me, it won't do any good. She is far easier to lead than to drive."

I was quite worn out when I reached my hotel, but despite all that had happened during the day I went to sleep with the firm conviction that everything would come right, and that the interview at the Hofburg would end all my anxiety about Mary and Rudolph. I did not remember that Fate holds the strings, and that we like children move.

CHAPTER XIII
THE CROWN PRINCE RETURNS ALONE

The morning after the storm - Mary's toilet - The green tailor-made costume - Good-bye for ever - The door in the wall - On the roof of the Hofburg - The end of the passage - The room of the raven - Rudolph's private apartments - Ten minutes - I discover where I am - Rudolph returns without Mary - Where is she? - I receive my instructions - The way back - What the coachman said

I awoke next morning with the feeling that something excessively disagreeable was in store for me. There is no time so conducive to depression as the hours before dawn, but in summer one's worries fly before the advent of the bright new day, whereas in winter-time they are not so easily banished. "O for the sunshine and warmth of the South!" I said to myself, and then I realised that the Riviera with the Vetseras would be perfectly impossible. "George must go to Biarritz instead," I reflected. "He won't be difficult to persuade when I tell him that the Baroness and her daughters meditate staying in the same place as ourselves."

I was punctual in keeping my appointment with Mary, and precisely at eleven o'clock I arrived at the Vetsera Palace, where I found the Baroness and Hannah in the boudoir. Madame Vetsera was crocheting woollen articles for the poor, while Hannah, as usual, was taken up with her painting, and everything looked so peaceful and homelike that I felt inclined to believe the tempestuous events of the previous evening were a dream.

I chatted on various subjects, but carefully avoided any mention of the domestic imbroglio. However, there was no sign of Mary, and I was impatient to get the visit to the Hofburg over and done with. I turned to Hannah: "Where's Mary? Isn't she dressed? I particularly said that I should fetch her at eleven o'clock."

Hannah did not raise her head from her work. "Oh, she has been locked in her room for the last two hours. I'm sure I don't know what she is doing. It is really better to leave Mary alone when she is so strange."

I seized this last straw which might happily prevent the interview I dreaded.

"If Mary is not herself," I said, rising as I spoke, "won't it be wiser for her not to go out?"

At this instant the sly pale face of Agnes appeared at the door. "Will Madame la Comtesse come to the Baroness Mary?" she asked; "the Baroness is almost dressed."

I followed Agnes. Mary was seated in front of her mirror, and she smiled at me in the glass as I entered. Her hair was simply dressed, and her whole appearance was so fresh and virginal that she looked more like an innocent young *fiancée* than the passion-tossed woman of the last few days, and I felt relieved to think that Rudolph would meet her in this quieter mood.

Mary wore a tight-fitting olive-green tailor-made costume, braided in black, and, as she fastened the collar with a simple gold brooch, she told me that she would not keep me waiting very much longer. She then went over to her bureau, which she locked, and put the key in her pocket. Mary wore no jewellery except her earrings, the iron bangle and ring, and a gold cross round her neck. I remarked on this, but she smiled and made no reply.

Agnes brought her hat, a creation of green felt, profusely trimmed with black ostrich feathers, and Mary put on a black veil, which she tied under her chin. She wore a sealskin coat, with a muff to match, and I thought that she had never looked so handsome. Mary kissed her mother good-bye in an undemonstrative way, but once outside the boudoir, her indifference vanished, and she ran downstairs and jumped into the fiacre. I followed more leisurely, but when we had started I noticed that. She was feverishly excited.

"Alas for my peaceful interview!" I thought, as I placed my hand on her shoulder. "Mary, I want to say something to you. Do you quite understand that I am acting treacherously to my aunt and uncle by taking you to meet the Crown Prince at the Hofburg?"

She was silent. "Try and realise that this weakness of mine is an act of pure friendship," I continued. "I can't bear to see you unhappy, but I am sure Rudolph will tell you what is best for you. Do as he says, and, take my advice, finish this episode; otherwise, I fear the results of it will be disastrous for us all."

Mary looked at me, and I shall never forget the expression in her beautiful eyes; an almost sublime love shone in their blue depths; but still she did not speak, and only a hand-pressure showed me that she had heard my words.

The fiacre stopped at the "White Cat," a shop famous for lingerie, where we got out, and I began to make purchases; but Mary was so impatient that there was nothing for it but to go back to our fiacre. I directed the man to stop in the street behind the palace of the Archduke Albert, and after telling him to wait until we returned, Mary and I walked in the direction of the entrance in the Burg wall.

We were evidently expected, for the little iron door was ajar. Mary pushed it open, and we saw Loschek, the Prince's valet, standing well inside the passage. He did not speak, but made a sign for us to follow him up flight after flight of steep dark stairs.

I could hardly see where I was going, and was almost breathless when our guide suddenly stopped and threw open a door which disclosed daylight at last.

We found ourselves on what I realised to be the flat roof of the Hofburg, and I could not help examining our surroundings with some interest, as from where we stood we had a magnificent view of Vienna, and the cold strong wind which swept the lofty spot almost carried us off our feet.

Loschek led the way across the roof, and a mad impulse to laugh seized me as I wondered what Aunt Cissi would say if she only knew who was traversing this overhead route to her son's apartments. I glanced at Mary: the wind had crimsoned her pale cheeks and loosened delightful little tendrils of her hair. All at once I felt in the grip of a fear which was beyond me to fathom and my subconscious self seemed struggling to warn me against some unknown danger. I stopped. Was it too late for retreat?

Mary saw my hesitation, and gripped my hand convulsively. "No, no, no. I will see Rudolph; you shall never prevent me doing so now."

Loschek watched us with blasé indifference. Doubtless in his time, he had escorted many hesitating ladies across the roof, and it was no novelty to him. He led the way to a window, through which we climbed down into the corridor below, and once more we were almost in darkness. I was dreadfully nervous. "Where are we going?" I inquired, and then the idea struck me that Mary seemed strangely well acquainted with the way.

I was inwardly raging at my folly in having participated in this adventure, when Loschek opened a door at the end of the passage, and I followed Mary inside. Something came out of the shadows with a whirr of wings, and flapped round my head. I gave a stifled scream, as I could not at first see what the something was. Then I felt two ice-cold claws on my neck, and a hoarse croak broke the stillness.

"It's only a tame raven," observed Mary impatiently. "Come here," and she lifted the bird off me, calling it by name as she did so.

"Poor fellow," she said, caressing the bird. "Why you *are* a coward, Marie; he's quite harmless, and rather a dear."

"He may be harmless," I answered crossly, "but I dislike having my nerves upset any more. I hope to goodness we are nearly at Rudolph's apartments."

The abode of the raven was a gunroom hung with quantities of antlers and trophies of the chase. The place opened into a vestibule, at the end of which I noticed some big double doors. Loschek flung these apart, and we entered a beautiful anteroom decorated in white and gold.

Mary walked up and down impatiently for some moments; then she came to me. Tears were in her eyes; she was pale, and seemed filled with some desperate resolve. She took both my hands in hers, and kissed me. Then she said very quietly and sadly:

"Marie, I want you to forgive me from the bottom of your heart for all the trouble which I have caused you. Whatever happens, don't think I wished to deceive you, or to play you false."

I was touched by her evident affection, and told her that I only wanted her to be happy, and that I should be well pleased if her ultimate peace of mind resulted from this interview.

Just then the door at the other end of the room opened, and the Crown Prince advanced to meet us.

Rudolph, who wore a mess jacket, looked quite cheerful, and smiled as he exchanged greetings with us. "Come into my own room," he said, "we shall be far more comfortable there."

He led the way into a cheerful apartment, which looked as if it were "lived in," for there was an abundance of illustrated papers, plenty of books and flowers, and a grand piano which was strewn with new music. A pair of spectacles was lying on the writing-table, and I wondered why Stéphanie had left her glasses there, since she and Rudolph were not popularly supposed to be on visiting terms.

"Now," said my cousin, in a most prosaic tone, "I want to have this little interview alone with Mary in the smoking-room. Will you permit this, Marie?"

"Oh, don't leave here," I replied, vaguely apprehensive of trouble, "I'll go back into the anteroom."

"Nonsense," answered Rudolph, "some one might see you if you wait there. I promise you I'll detain the Baroness only ten minutes." He opened the door, and before I could say a word Mary slipped past me and was gone. The Crown Prince followed her. "Only *ten minutes*," he repeated, as he closed the door, and I heard him turn the key in the lock.

I was powerless to interfere, and walked over to the windows to see if I could discover in what part of the Burg I was. To my surprise I saw that the windows looked out over the Amalienhof, and that immediately opposite me were the Empress's apartments, which I knew so well. I could see the big clock, and I heard the rumble of the carriages which passed and repassed through the courtyard below.

I watched the busy scene for a little time, then glanced at the clock - the ten minutes had already passed.

I went to the mirror and smoothed my hair, which had been disarranged by the raven's sudden swoop, and as I did so I heard the sound of military music. It was the hour for changing the guard. The room was unpleasantly warm, and I took off my jacket, but hardly had I done so when my cousin entered. *He was alone.*

I stared at Rudolph in dismay, and could only stammer, "Where's Mary?"

He smiled, but took no notice of my question, and then proceeded to lock all the doors in the room.

"Speak to me," I cried; "for goodness' sake tell me what has happened. Rudolph, explain yourself."

I was so terrified that I could hardly stand. The blood rushed to my head; I swayed and trembled, and the room swam before my eyes.

The Crown Prince took my hand. "There is nothing to explain," he said.

"Mary! Mary! where is she? Oh, do tell me what you have done with her ..."

"Calm yourself, Marie, and listen to me. Now don't interrupt. You will have to return without Mary."

The sounds of the gay music outside rose and fell as we were speaking, and I never hear a military band without recalling that awful moment. I turned sick with fear. "You are joking; you don't know what you are saying; you cannot surely mean to tell me that you intend to keep Mary here?"

"Never mind where I intend to keep Mary; all you have to do is to go home at once."

His callous indifference infuriated me - "I will *not* go home without her."

"You must. Mary is not in the Burg."

The shock almost paralysed me. Then I came to myself. My cousin continued: "Nothing will happen if you will keep quiet. Go back to the Baroness and say that Mary has run away."

"Oh, you coward, Rudolph. I won't. I'll go direct to the Empress."

"You cannot pass through locked doors."

I rushed to the window, tried to throw it open, and shouted for help.

The Prince violently put his hand over my mouth and dragged me back. "Do you want me to hurt you?" he asked with dreadful meaning in his voice.

"Oh, you dishonourable man," I panted, "you are lost to all shame. I won't be silent, I will tell the Empress, let me go ... you must ... you *shall*."

"Unless you swear to be quiet, I'll *kill* you," hissed Rudolph. He released my wrists, which he held as in a vice, and without another word opened a drawer in his writing-table and took from it a little black revolver. He came to where I stood.

"Do you want me to shoot you?" He caught me by the throat and pressed the weapon against my forehead.

"Yes, shoot me," I answered miserably. "It would be a kind thing to do now that you have ruined my life."

The Crown Prince put down the revolver, and looked at me. "At any rate, you have some courage," he observed.

"I can be brave when I have to face devils like you," I cried. "For you are nothing but a devil. You brought me here under a solemn promise to deal with me in an honourable way; you do not know the meaning of the word. Yes, I repeat it, you do not know the meaning of honour."

The Crown Prince glanced at me with mingled cruelty and cynicism. "Since when, may I ask, Marie, have you been considered fit to play the saint? You are a fine one to talk of honour or loyalty. You have been the go-between for my mother since you were a girl. And yet you dare to mention morality to me, when you have not scrupled to stand by and see my father deceived."

"It is a monstrous lie. I'll not listen - you shall not traduce your mother. I love her."

Then I burst into tears, and cried as if my heart would break. Whereupon Rudolph said very quietly.

"Marie, do you really love mamma? Well, if you do, save her from the shame which a scandal will cause her."

To my great surprise, he led me over to the couch and sat down beside me. "Yes, you are quite right," he observed, with a complete change in his manner. "Yes - I have treated you very badly. Marie, can you ever forgive me?"

"Oh ... h ... h ... h ..." was my only reply.

"I must have been mad. ... Will you listen? I beg of you to give me a hearing. It rests with you alone to avert a tragedy."

"How can I believe you?"

"I swear to you by the Black Virgin of the Burg that I will speak the truth. I want to keep Mary with me for two days in order to come to an easy understanding with the Baroness over her."

"Oh, but you are mad," I said. "You told me you had no time for love, that there were matters which you dared not disregard, and yet after telling me this you abduct a young girl. I don't believe you. It's all a string of falsehoods."

"It is the truth. A great deal may happen in two days, and I want Mary to be with me. I stand on the edge of a precipice. Why should you grudge me a little happiness?" queried Rudolph.

"Mary also said these words to me," I replied - "but what you term happiness is not the real thing. I don't think people like you ever experience it."

"Give me one last chance," he pleaded.

"Well, I can but hear what you wish me to do."

"I want you to go back to your fiacre, and tell the man to drive you to some shop where you are well known as a customer. Once you are inside send an assistant out to the fiacre with a message from you to the Baroness Mary Vetsera. Naturally, he will return, and say the Baroness is not there. You will thus be able to produce a witness to testify that you thought she was."

"But the coachman will know that I came out of the Burg alone."

The Crown Prince opened a leather wallet and took from it a roll of notes. "Here's five hundred florins," he said; "give them to

170

the coachman, with the message that I sent them, and that if any trouble arises he must go to Bratfisch, who will tell him what to do."

"And I am to tell her mother that Mary ran away when I was inside the shop?"

"Yes," replied Rudolph, "it will serve for two days, and then I shall see her myself."

"You will not find her difficult to persuade," I said, and I repeated the conversation which I had had with Madame Vetsera.

The Crown Prince laughed. "What an accommodating mother Mary possesses," he observed. "Now, Marie, you must go. ... Will you have some wine? ... My poor cousin, you look a complete wreck."

I refused the wine. I was still crying, but I longed to be gone. I was in a dreadful state of nervous exhaustion, and my faculties were completely numbed; my one wish was to get away.

Rudolph suddenly took my hand. "Don't let us part in anger, Marie," he entreated. "Oh, if you only knew how unhappy I am. ... Perhaps it will come all right ... one day. Promise me you will be true to your trust."

"I promise," I answered in a stifled voice.

The Crown Prince drew me to him, and took me in his arms. Then he kissed me for the first and last time.

I walked through the anteroom as if I were dreaming, and found myself again in the Abode of the Raven. Loschek silently took me back across the roof and down the staircase to the door in the wall. As it closed I felt that I had left the greater part of my life behind me.

When I got back to where the fiacre was waiting, I found the coachman eating a thick cheese sandwich, and the horses had their nose bags on. Evidently he had anticipated a long wait.

The man, who had driven me for years, was quite struck by my altered appearance, but I quickly gave him Rudolph's orders, and handed him the notes. "Far too much to spend on a lady," he remarked; It's an expensive love affair that costs the Crown Prince five hundred florins."

I drove away more dead than alive, but with a tremendous effort I pulled myself together, and when I went to Rodeck's in the Kohlmarkt everything passed off without arousing any suspicion. I displayed great anxiety when Mary was reported to be missing, and hurried out of the shop at once. "Drive me to the Vetsera Palace as quickly as possible," I said in a distinct voice.

CHAPTER XIV
THE TRAGEDY OF MAYERLING

I break the news of Mary's flight - "No scandal" - What did the Baroness suspect? – I promise to discover Rudolph's whereabouts - A family council - Alexandre Baltazzi – A visit to the Chief of the Secret Police - "I cannot interfere" - I am recalled to Pardubitz - Home again - A dreadful awakening - The Crown Prince is dead - "How?" - And what of Mary? - My legacy from the dead - I fear the future - Who will reclaim the box?

I entered the Vetsera Palace in a most unenviable frame of mind. I felt really ill, and my knees trembled under me as I slowly walked up the staircase. An appetising smell of well-cooked food issued from the dining-room as Hannah came out to meet me. "Mamma was so hungry that we started lunch without you," she said; then when she noticed how worried I looked she was silent and waited for me to speak.

"Hannah ... ask your mother to come to me. ... Don't lose an instant."

I walked almost mechanically into the smoking-room, and threw myself on the couch, hardly knowing what I did. The door opened and Madame Vetsera rushed in, napkin in hand, "Whatever is wrong? Are you ill?" she exclaimed.

"Mary has run away; I have come back without her ..." I scarcely recognised my own voice as I uttered these words so fraught with fatality, and I looked at the Baroness with a kind of fearful fascination to see how the news would affect her.

Madame Vetsera turned pale, bit her lips, and said in a colourless voice:

"I was certain that she would do *something* rash."

Hannah, who had followed her mother, seemed unable to speak; the Baroness burst into tears, and I struggled to overcome my own emotions. I remembered Rudolph's remark that the Baroness was "an accommodating mother," and thought that her words savoured more of wounded ambition, than the despairing cry of maternal love.

Madame Vetsera dried her tears, and attempted to regain her composure. "Tell me all that has happened."

I played the role assigned to me by Rudolph, and forced myself to tell untruth after untruth, but at length I lost my nerve completely and broke into a storm of tears and self-reproaches.

"Don't distress yourself," said the Baroness; "it is not your fault, Mary was impossible. You can't imagine the life I have had with her - but it is an unpardonable action on *his* part," she added, with an access of sudden passion in her voice.

"Hélène," I answered, breathlessly, "do you then connect the Crown Prince with Mary's flight?"

"Yes," replied Madame Vetsera, her eyes sparkling with anger. "Yes, I suspect a great deal, but it is only lately that I have heard things."

A heavy weight seemed lifted off my heart. I was not alone responsible for the consequences of this intrigue, since Mary's mother was admittedly cognisant of it. "What shall we do?" I asked.

"Nothing, just now," replied the Baroness. "Let us wait and see whether she will return. I will not have any scandal, it would be fatal to our position in Vienna. Everything must be hushed up; we must see that the servants do not gossip; I can rely on old Christian, and the concierge is also trustworthy. Agnes - oh, but Agnes!" cried Madame Vetsera, "I'm sure she is at the bottom of it all, and I will settle with her later. At present the main thing to remember is the necessity for silence."

She said this last sentence in an undertone, and then my absolutely dejected appearance seemed to strike her afresh, for I think I must have looked like a living corpse. "Do have something," she insisted; "you seem dreadfully ill; I'll order some wine," and so saying Madame Vetsera went into the dining-room.

Hannah, who had left us unobserved, now returned, holding in one hand a piece of paper and in the other a small jewel-case. She was just about to speak when her mother came back, followed by Christian, who offered me a glass of wine and some biscuits.

Hannah gave the slip of paper to the Baroness, who read it aloud: "Dear mother, when you get this I shall be in the Danube - Mary."

"What folly!" I cried. "Mary is alive and well; she only wants to prevent her place of concealment being discovered."

"Absolutely," assented the Baroness. Hannah turned to her mother: "Mary has left all her jewellery inside a silver box on her toilette table, the writing-table drawers are empty, and there is only this box," she said, giving the case to her mother.

"Let us force the lock," I suggested: "perhaps the clue to the mystery is inside."

Christian broke open the box, but it was empty except for the photograph of a child, which I recognised as Rudolph at the age of three.

After I had drunk the wine I felt a little better, and we discussed Mary's disappearance and Madame Vetsera's wish to avoid scandal. The dread of gossip seemed to affect her far more than the loss of her daughter, and I could not help feeling sorry for Mary when I saw how little real affection her mother seemed to have for her.

"Will you do me the greatest favour possible?" asked Madame Vetsera, when I rose to take my departure.

"Yes, willingly," I replied.

"Then go to the Hofburg, and ask for news of the Crown Prince; you are his cousin, and they can't refuse to tell you. There is something else ... can you possibly put off going back to Pardubitz for twenty-four hours? We shall surely have news between then and now."

I hesitated. I could not face another visit to the Burg ... still I could send my maid; but as to delaying my return, that was quite another thing, as I had to consider my husband. However, I felt that it was my duty to do everything in my power for the Baroness, more especially as I was the innocent cause of all the trouble.

"Very well," I said, "I will inquire at the Burg, and remain in Vienna another day."

The Baroness kissed me, and thanked me. I said "Good-bye" to Hannah, and drove off to my hotel where I was delighted to find Madame Muller, who had, doubtless, come on the chance of my telling her what had happened on the previous evening. Faithful to my promise to Madame Vetsera, I despatched Jenny at once to the Hofburg, and asked Madame Muller to send a telegram to Pardubitz. "Come back if you've nothing better to do," I said to her, "I'm all nerves and I hate my own society."

I waited anxiously for Jenny, and when she returned, I gathered that the Crown Prince was shooting at Laxenburg, a story which I knew was perfectly untrue. As I felt more composed I thought I would go and tell the Baroness what I had heard, and I also hoped that by this time Mary had done something to relieve her mother's anxiety.

When I arrived at the Vetsera Palace, I found myself in the midst of a family council, as the Baroness had sent for Alexandre Baltazzi, who was perfectly furious over his niece's behaviour. Hannah, whose face was swollen with crying, tried to calm her uncle, and Madame Vetsera seemed to have lost her head completely under the storm of her brother's angry reproaches. Alexandre declared that he would speak to the Crown Prince face to face and force him to explain matters, but the Baroness insisted with sobs and tears that there must be no scandal, and I joined my entreaties to hers.

"Very well," said Alexandre, "I will not go after the Crown Prince, but I must know where he is to be found. You, Countess, as a member of the family can ask questions impossible for us. Will you go with me to see the Chief of the Secret Police? He will be certain to know where your cousin is and we need not tell him anything about Mary unless it is absolutely necessary."

"We shall have to," I said quietly; but although I spoke without displaying any emotion, I was almost too miserable for words. Bad and treacherous as Rudolph was, I did not wish to put anyone on his track, especially as he might be actively engaged in his mysterious political intrigues.

I was puzzled at Madame Vetsera's attitude, for since she considered Rudolph to be the abductor of her daughter, why was she so averse to bringing him to book? I could only put it down to her sensitiveness about the honour of her family; but then as Mary had remarked, "The history of the virtuous Vetseras was well-known in society."

"Listen," I said to Alexandre, after what seemed an interminable discussion, "I'll accompany you, but please behave with discretion. I do not like being mixed up in Rudolph's discreditable affairs; you must know that I have others to consider beside myself, and I don't want to quarrel with the Empress."

We drove to the préfecture, a dull and depressing place which seemed encompassed with mystery and crime. I sent in my card with a request for an interview, and we were ushered into the presence of the Chief of the Secret Police, a grave-looking man who seemed surprised at our late visit.

Directly I told the Chief that I was related to the Empress, he was instantly on the alert, and I briefly explained that I wished to ascertain the present whereabouts of the Crown Prince, who had persuaded a young lady to leave her home and to accompany him. "The honour of a well-known name is at stake," I said; "there must be no scandal, and the chief object is to persuade the girl to return to her mother at once."

The Chief of the Police listened to me in silence until I had finished speaking. "I cannot possibly interfere," he replied emphatically, "it is not within my province, for believe me, Countess, that if I were to mix myself up in the love affairs of the Imperial House I should have my hands full. Indeed," he added, "I dare not."

Alexandre Baltazzi thereupon lost his temper.

"What! are the Habsburgs allowed to behave like common ravishers and yet go unpunished ⁃ is there no justice in Vienna?" he cried angrily.

"I cannot interfere with what the Crown Prince chooses to do," repeated the Chief of the Police.

"But perhaps you don't realise," said I, "that this young lady belongs to the aristocracy."

"Then it's not one of the *bourgeoisie*? Oh, that's *quite* another story," replied the functionary. "Very well, I will see what I can do," and he left the room whilst we waited in suspense for his return.

"His Imperial Highness is at Alland," announced the Chief when he came back a quarter of an hour later, and the polite bow which accompanied his words intimated that the interview was at an end.

As we left the préfecture I asked Alexandre if he knew where Alland was. He replied that it was within easy distance of Vienna, and when we acquainted the Baroness, she decided that she would go to Alland the next day and insist on seeing Mary and the Crown Prince.

Half dead with worry and fatigue, I returned to my hotel, where I found Madame Muller waiting in my bedroom. A telegram had arrived. I tore it open with trembling fingers, and was mortified to read a curt message from my husband. The Count positively forbade me to put off my departure a day longer!

There was nothing for it but to return to Pardubitz at once. I enclosed the telegram in a letter to Madame Vetsera, and asked her to send me all news under cover to Jenny. The Baroness wrote an affectionate note in reply, and told me that she would wire or write directly she received any tidings of Mary.

The next morning I left Vienna by the first train!

I had never before been so glad to return to my quiet home! It seemed like a haven of rest after the storm of passions through which I had. passed. But the journey to Pardubitz was not pleasant. I was the prey of bitter self-reproaches and more than once I was tempted to tell the Count everything; but I felt that if I did I should never hear the last of my indiscretion, and so I decided not to unburden my mind to him. Although I possess some strength of character, I was always childishly afraid of incurring my husband's anger, and I rarely confided in him, more especially when the trouble concerned one of my relations. Why had I been so criminally weak? I asked myself; and then with positive terror I remembered the dreadful steel box. What could it contain? Rudolph had said "papers," and I argued that by papers he might possibly have meant his correspondence with Mary Vetsera.

The voice of the train seemed to repeat two names, "Rudolph," "Mary," with monotonous insistence, and I endeavoured to distract my mind by looking at the flying landscape, which was lightly powdered with snow; but the dreariness of the winter scene only served to depress me further, and I was glad when I reached Pardubitz.

The first night at home came as a real blessing, for I was absolutely worn out. I slept the dreamless sleep of utter exhaustion, and felt decidedly better and brighter when I awoke. I had confided in Jenny, and it was a great relief to talk to her, for she was so devoted and honest that I knew my secret was in safe keeping.

Count Larisch commented on my loss of spirits and remarked that the visit to Vienna had made me look very ill. "But," he said, "I am far from well myself, and have decided to start for Mentone at once; we shall not stay in Vienna, but go straight through and break the journey on the Naprasina frontier."

I was very busy with my preparations and waited anxiously for news from the Baroness Vetsera, but none came, so I sent her a letter to say we were only at Pardubitz for twenty hours, and that I would write from Monte Carlo.

I went to bed early on the evening of January 30th, and was fast asleep when Jenny came into my room next morning and pulled back the heavy window-curtains. The fire had not been lit, and, shivering, I drew the eiderdown quilt closer over me, and at the same time said rather crossly:

"Why have you awakened me so early?"

"Madame la Comtesse," answered Jenny in a voice so changed that I could hardly believe it was she who was speaking, "a dreadful thing has happened. My God ... how can I tell you?" She fell on her knees beside the bed. "How *can* I tell you?" she repeated, "I'm afraid."

"Speak, Jenny, tell me at once," I cried.

"Oh, Madame, the Crown Prince has been killed."

I looked at her, scarcely comprehending the dreadful import of her words. I was tongue-tied.

"Yes, yes," sobbed Jenny, "the baker has just brought the news, but it was rumoured in Pardubitz late last night. They say his Imperial Highness was accidentally shot whilst out shooting."

"Where? At Alland?" I managed to stammer, for my mouth was dry and I could hardly speak.

"No ... at Mayerling," answered the weeping maid.

I sprang out of bed; my blood seemed to turn to ice; my one idea was to go to my husband, but Jenny begged me to wait until breakfast, as the Count's valet was with him.

I do not remember how I dressed on that dreadful morning, for I was not conscious of anything that went on. All I knew was that Rudolph was dead. Oh, how - by whose hand? I questioned Jenny, but she could give me no details. Then, with a sickening feeling at my heart, I remembered Mary. Where was she? What had happened to her; surely she had never killed her lover?

Ah ... the newspapers - they would be full of the tragedy. I rushed downstairs, and as I passed my husband's room I heard him talking to his valet about the catastrophe at Mayerling. The papers were lying on the breakfast-table, and I saw the heading "Death of the Crown Prince Rudolph." The pages were bordered with deep black lines, and over the heading was a cross!

The letters danced before my eyes, but I forced myself to read the report, which was a bare announcement, and contained no details whatever. A leading article deplored the loss which Austria-Hungary had sustained, but that was all.

I was nearly mad with terror and anguish, and hardly listened to my husband when he told me the news of Rudolph's death. Count Larisch was quite unmoved, and remarked that he had always anticipated a sudden end for my cousin. "It is a great nuisance that we shall be obliged to go to Vienna for the funeral," he said in aggrieved tones. He then ate a very good breakfast, whilst I felt as if every morsel would choke me, and at last I could sit at table no longer.

I found Jenny busy packing when I went back to my bedroom.

"I must send a telegram to the Baroness Vetsera," I said. "Be quick, you must go with it to the post-office." And I sat down at my writing-table.

"Oh, Madame la Comtesse," she replied, "forgive me if I tell you that it is unwise to do so. I beg you to wait until we get to Vienna. It is no use to set people talking at such a critical time."

I realised the truth of her remarks, and as I put down my pen my eyes fell on Mary's photograph, with the words she had written, "True till Death." Had they any sinister meaning? And I shrieked so dreadfully that my maid rushed to see what ailed me. Then I mercifully became unconscious.

But not for long; life with its perplexities recalled me, and then the stabbing knowledge pierced my tormented brain that the steel box and its secret was my legacy from the dead.

Late on that awful evening I nerved myself to open my trunk, and took out the mysterious box. Rudolph could never reclaim it now; but who would carry out his trust?

I was glad when the hour of our departure arrived, for the agony of mind which I suffered was almost beyond endurance. I felt like a traveller in an unknown country who is beset with hidden dangers, and walks fearful that his next step will lead him into ambush. I could' have welcomed death, for I feared what lay before me. The image of the dead man haunted me. I recalled our last meeting, and although I was firmly convinced that I was destined to suffer through his selfish duplicity, I was glad I had not refused Rudolph a farewell kiss.

CHAPTER XV
NARRATIVE OF THE COURT PHYSICIAN

*A city of sorrow - Haunted by memories - The hair of the Furies -
The bells – One-two-three - Dr. Wiederhofer - An emissary from the
Empress - What the doctor told me - Mayerling - How Rudolph died
- The news at the Hofburg - The two mothers – "Ils sont morts tous
les deux" - The linen room - The body in the basket - Mary – "Take
her up tenderly" - A visit from Count Stockau - The Baroness
Vetsera is ordered to leave Vienna - Alexandre Baltazzi and Count
Stockau proceed to Mayerling - The last toilette of Mary Vetsera - A
dreadful drive - The burial-ground of Heiligenkreuz – The rough
coffin - Buried like a dog - I receive Mary's last letter*

We travelled at night, and when we arrived at Vienna we found a
city of sorrow. I cannot describe my feelings when I saw the black
crowds and the signs of universal mourning; a sombre stillness
hung like a funeral pall over everything and everybody, and there
was a sense of horror and mystery in the very air we breathed.

When we entered the Grand Hotel I was surprised to find that
people stared and whispered as I passed; for I was not then aware
that the thousand tongues of slander had already begun to busy
themselves concerning me.

I felt an icy shiver when I found myself back in my old room
where the passionate drama of the last few days had been enacted.
I thought I saw Mary's lovely despairing face, I heard Rudolph's
hurried breathing, and listened to his wild words. There was the
couch where we had sat when he gave me the steel box. This was
Mary's chair when she listened to what she termed "my sermon.
"Yes, I could almost smell the odour of her cigarette and hear the
impatient click, click of her little high heels. Oh, it was terrible!

Where was Mary? Why could I hear nothing of her? I could bear the suspense no longer, and after breakfast I sent Jenny to the Vetsera Palace. I was vaguely uneasy, as there was no message from the Empress, who knew of our arrival in Vienna, and the only person who had inquired for me was Dr. Wiederhofer, who left a message that he would call on urgent business during the afternoon.

The Count went out to see his family, and I waited anxiously for Jenny's return, but I was astounded when she said that the Vetsera Palace was shut up. Mistress and servants had gone and the house-boy who was in charge could give no information whatever.

"Oh, Madame la Comtesse," cried Jenny, "what does it all mean? Yesterday Prince A.'s valet, who travelled with me, told me his master had heard that the Crown Prince had not been accidentally shot, but had been killed in the forest! What is one to believe?"

I could not answer. I walked over to the window, but recoiled in horror when I saw the black flags and crêpe streamers waving in the street. The twisting ribbons seemed to me like the black serpents which entwine the hair of the Furies, and I instinctively repeated the words, "Say by which Fury ... are you tormented?" My soul was in anguish; my nerves rebelled against the strain imposed upon them; I wanted to scream, to dash myself against the wall ... anything. ... I clenched my hands, and the nails pierced my flesh; no tears came to relieve my burning eyes; my throat was parched - oh, what *could* I do?

And then the air outside vibrated with the deep and solemn tolling of bells. Each stroke made my heart quiver, and fell like a sledgehammer on my tired brain. Would they never stop? One - two - three - Rudolph was now lying in the Augustina Kirche ... where was his spirit? Near me, I felt sure ... what touched my cheek just then? ... the last kiss ... yes, that's what I felt ... one - two - three - the bells again; I shall hear them for ever in my dreams.

I flung myself on the couch; I put my fingers in my ears to deaden the haunting noise; I buried my head in the cushions; I felt I should die if I had much more to bear.

I started all at once, for a hand had been laid upon my shoulder. My eyes met the calm gaze of my old friend and physician, Dr. Wiederhofer. He pressed my hand reassuringly. "Calm yourself, dear Countess," he said, "for you must listen attentively to what I have to say. I am sent here by the Empress."

"Does Aunt Cissi wish to see me?" I asked.

"No, she wishes you to answer a question. What do you know about this affair?"

"I know nothing, I'm nearly dead with anxiety. For pity's sake, tell *me* something."

"You are certain that you are speaking the truth."

"I swear it."

"Then, my poor friend ... prepare yourself ... Mary is dead."

"Oh, my God!" I cried. "How did she die?"

"With the Crown Prince. Countess ... a little fortitude ... you are shaking like a leaf. ... So ‑ that's better. Yes, they are both dead; and the Empress thinks it is owing to you. I pity you, my poor child, for you are in a dreadful predicament," said the doctor, and his voice faltered as he spoke.

"But I am innocent," I cried.

"Everything is known at the Burg," he said gravely. "The secret police have discovered that you were in Rudolph's confidence, and that you took Mary Vetsera to the Hofburg. The man who drove you there has confessed all. But, I beseech you, tell me what the Empress chiefly wishes to know. *Was* the Crown Prince perfectly normal at your last interview?"

I nerved myself to reply, "No, he was not." Then my pent‑up misery burst forth. "You say they know all at the Burg. Do the Emperor and Empress realise that I have been treated shamefully? I have been the cat's paw in this affair. I've been deceived throughout ... I'll see the Empress. I won't be condemned unjustly." My voice rose to a scream and died away in convulsive sobbing.

Dr. Wiederhofer let me cry for some moments.

"Courage, courage, dear Countess; I am convinced that you have spoken the truth. I had better tell you all that has happened. But it is a dreadful story.

"The Crown Prince wrote to Laxenburg, it appears," said the doctor, "and told his wife he was going for three days' shooting to Mayerling but that he would return for the family dinner on January 30th. There was consequently no anxiety felt about his movements, and the Prince left Vienna two hours after Mary Vetsera, who was driven to the shooting lodge by Bratfisch. The unhappy girl went in unnoticed by the private entrance, and Loschek took her to the little dressing-room in the apartments which the Crown Prince occupied. She remained that day and night alone with her lover, and on the 29th some of Rudolph's friends came for the shooting."

"Was Philip of Coburg among them?"

"He was. Philip," continued Dr. Wiederhofer, "knew that a woman was at Mayerling (it was no rare event) because on such occasions Rudolph never sat long at dinner. The Crown Prince, who pleaded a bad cold, did not go out with the guns, and that evening he sat at table with his throat muffled in a silk handkerchief.

"Supper was served to the Prince and Mary in their apartments, and Loschek received instructions to awaken his master at seven o'clock the next morning.

"Downstairs a drunken orgy prevailed, but those two sinful souls spent their last night undisturbed."

"Oh, for pity's sake be brief, I cannot bear it!" I sobbed.

"You must hear everything," replied my friend. "Loschek came to waken his master at seven o'clock, and the Crown Prince told him to return in half an hour. He did so, but as there was no answer to his repeated knocking he became alarmed and sent for Count Hoyos, who was at breakfast."

"And ... what happened?"

"They broke open the door, and I hope they may never see such a sight again. There was blood everywhere. It stained the pillows, it bespattered the walls, and it had flowed in a sluggish stream from the bed to the floor, where it had made a horrible pool. Rudolph lay on his side, his hand still holding the revolver, and the top of his head was almost completely shattered."

"I cannot listen ..."

"Countess ... it is imperative that you should hear all. The bed bulged a little and Count Hoyos lifted the coverings. Mary Vetsera lay under them - dead; she too had been shot in the head."

"Oh, Mary, Mary! Poor Mary!" I cried in agony.

"Count Hoyos told Loschek to take the body of the girl into another room, and to lock all the doors of the death chamber. The Count then went downstairs and informed the shooters that the Crown Prince had been suddenly taken ill, and that he must leave for Vienna at once to acquaint the Emperor, and to bring a doctor back to Mayerling. He despatched a telegram to me, and I arrived at the Hofburg almost at the same time as he did.

"We saw the Empress first; she had just finished her gymnastics ... It was dreadful to find her so unprepared. I cannot tell you how we broke the news to her . ...."

"Oh, my poor, poor aunt!'

"The Empress seemed like a woman suddenly turned to stone. She shed no tears; all she said was, 'How can we tell the Emperor?'

"I found strength to say, You must tell him, your Majesty - you alone can.' The Empress stared at me almost without comprehension. Then she started, and shivered a little. '*Well, let us go,*' she said.

"We walked with the Empress to the Emperor's apartments, and waited outside. I do not know what passed between the bereaved parents, but when we were called in Francis-Joseph sat by the table with his face hidden in his hands, and the Empress stood beside him.

"I received my orders to go to Mayerling at once. Count Hoyos gave me the key of the room on my arrival."

"What of the Empress?"

"When the Empress came back Madame Ferenzy told her that the Baroness Vetsera begged for an audience. The Baroness insisted that the Crown Prince had abducted her daughter and implored the Empress to help her.

"Elizabeth hesitated, and then told Madame Ferenzy that she would receive Madame Vetsera. The Empress stood in the middle of the anteroom; her whole aspect was terrible in its unnatural calm, and the Baroness was brought into her presence. The two mothers looked at each other in silence; then Madame Vetsera fell on her knees with a despairing cry, 'Mary - my daughter -'

"Elizabeth shrank back from the poor woman's outstretched arms. She examined her with pitiless curiosity, and then said coldly and cruelly, '*C'est trop tard. Ils sont morts tous les deux.*'

"Madame Vetsera fainted. The Empress looked at her unmoved, and walked away without a word."

I had listened to this terrible narration with indescribable emotions. I knew that my fate was sealed with regard to Aunt Cissi; she would never listen to any explanations of mine. I asked the doctor to continue his story, hardly knowing whether I should have strength to listen to it.

Wiederhofer went on to say that he had gone to Mayerling, and was taken immediately to the apartments occupied by the Crown Prince. Here he found everything much as Count Hoyos had described. The remains of supper were still on the table in the little salon; there were some empty champagne bottles, and one chair had been overturned.

A decanter half full of brandy lay on the carpet near the bed, and Wiederhofer ordered it to be removed to prevent the Emperor from seeing it. He then temporarily bandaged the shattered head and washed the face and neck of the Crown Prince. With the aid of Loschek he covered up the bloodstained bed, and made the body somewhat presentable; all else was left untouched to await the arrival of the Emperor.

"And now," said Loschek to Dr. Wiederhofer, "now you must see the woman." He preceded the doctor, and led the way down a corridor; he opened a door, and Wiederhofer found himself in a small room which was lit by a skylight. It was very difficult at first to distinguish the various objects around him, but at last the doctor saw a large linen basket. On the top of this was a hat trimmed with ostrich feathers, and the floor was strewn with various articles of woman's clothing.

Wiederhofer was well accustomed to horrible sights in the exercise of his profession, "but," he said, "for the first time in my career I felt faint when Loschek threw aside the sheet which covered the basket.

"There I saw the body of a woman - nude except for a fine lawn and lace chemise, which had been pulled up over her head. I told Loschek that it was too dark for me to examine the corpse where it was lying, so he carried it into the adjoining room and placed it on the billiard table.

"Then I began my examination. I parted the long hair away from the face, which was almost completely hidden, and then ... Oh, Countess! ... then I recognised Mary Vetsera - the girl I had known ever since she was a child."

The voice of the good doctor trembled with emotion. "Poor child," he said, "for she was little more than a child!"

Mary was not so terribly disfigured as Rudolph; part of her face was badly wounded and an eye had fallen out of its socket, but the uninjured side preserved all its beauty and her expression was almost peaceful.

Professor Wiederhofer tore the lawn chemise into strips for bandages; he then replaced the eye and bandaged the head; he washed Mary's face, and after wrapping the poor dead girl in a sheet he told Loschek to take her back to the linen room.

The scene in the chamber of death after the Emperor arrived at Mayerling was agonising. Francis-Joseph leant against the wall and cried as if his heart would break; then he listened to all that there was to tell, and afterwards returned to Vienna for the last home-coming of the Crown Prince.

"I refused to certify the cause of death as apoplexy," said the professor, indignantly, to me; "there has been far too much mystery made about the affair, and it will only raise a storm of popular feeling against the Emperor if the people of Austro-

Hungary are kept in the dark as to the cause of the Prince's death."

"Did my cousin leave any papers?" I asked with sudden apprehension.

"The Imperial Police have taken everything away. There were certain letters, I believe," replied Dr. Wiederhofer.

"Rudolph's body was embalmed," he added, "and placed in a coffin. It remained for some hours in the dining-room, and was removed to Vienna that evening."

"What has happened to poor Mary?"

"I cannot say," was the reply. "I was told that her relations were to fetch her body later."

I could not suppress my tears, when I pictured Mary's body left alone in such sordid surroundings. Poor darling I To think that she had perished by the hand of the man she adored.

Whither had their spirits flown? I seemed to move among a world of ghosts, and feel myself the shadow of a dream. Then I heard the sound of surging waters; I was engulfed by them, and remembered nothing more until I came to myself. Jenny was bathing my temples with eau de cologne, and Dr. Wiederhofer was bending anxiously over me.

"Courage, dear Countess," he whispered. "I must leave you now. I am due at the Hofburg. You may rely on me to do all in my power for you."

"Ask the Empress to receive me," I entreated, "that is all I wish. I have so much to tell her."

The kind doctor promised to use his influence, and then left me alone with Jenny.

I was not long permitted to enjoy rest for either body or mind. A knock came at the door. Jenny went to see who it was, and announced Mary's uncle, Count Stockau.

I could not refuse to see him, but I was greatly distressed at his changed appearance, for he looked absolutely bowed with trouble; in fact, I hardly recognised him. The Count had come to implore

189

me to reveal all I knew about the tragedy, and, like Dr. Wiederhofer, he was surprised to find I knew so little.

I asked what had become of Madame Vetsera.

"Ah, poor woman," exclaimed Count Stockau mournfully, "she has quitted Vienna for ever."

"By whose orders?" I asked.

"When my sister-in-law left the Hofburg, after her interview with the Empress, she returned home," replied the Count, "but almost immediately she received an intimation from the Imperial Geheimpolizei that under no circumstances was she to be permitted to see her daughter's body. She was further commanded to leave Austria at once for Venice, and from there to send a notice to the newspapers of Mary's sudden death in that city."

"What tyranny!" I ejaculated. "But tell me, where is Mary buried?"

Count Stockau, who was quite overcome with emotion, told me that on the evening of January 30th, he and Alexandre Baltazzi received instructions that they were to proceed at once in a closed carriage to Mayerling. One of the secret police sat beside the coachman, and on their arrival they were taken to the linen room where Mary's body was still lying in the basket.

The uncles were then told that the orders were that the corpse of the Baroness Mary was to be fully dressed and taken to the carriage which was waiting. "And," said the policeman, "you are to support the body between you in such a way as to make it appear that the Baroness still lives."

Then began the dreadful task of dressing the dead. Mary's hair was smoothed and pinned up in one heavy twist, and the uncles who loved her tenderly washed away the fresh stains on the once beautiful face. Then a ghastly thing occurred. Wiederhofer's lawn bandage broke ... But much endurance was mercifully given to the two gentlemen, and Count Stockau bound up the wound with his black silk cravat.

Mary was dressed in her underlinen and corsets; her silk stockings and dainty boots were put on, and then came the pretty gown she had worn on that disastrous day at the Hofburg. Her hat and veil were next placed on her head, and the body was set in a chair until her uncles could nerve themselves to wrap her in her sealskin oat.

It must have been an awful experience for those who assisted at this last toilette of Mary Vetsera, for as her uncles were preparing to put on the coat her head drooped heavily on her breast and she could not, of course, be taken out like that.

The police officer at once thought of an expedient, and he slipped a walking-stick down the dead girl's back, and bound her neck to the stick with a handkerchief. Count Stockau and Alexandre Baltazzi then put on the fur coat and lifted the corpse off the chair.

The two men supported their niece's body between them, and half carried it and half dragged it out of the room, along the dimly lit corridor, and down the principal staircase to the waiting carriage.

The dead girl was placed on the back seat, and her uncles sat opposite. Count Stockau told me that occasionally the jolting threw Mary almost upon them, and he said that her close contact during this sinister journey was almost more than they could bear.

It was a cold, windy night; from time to time the face of the moon was hidden by the flying clouds, and as the frost quite obscured the windows, it was impossible to see in what direction they were proceeding. At last the carriage stopped before a dark iron-barred door, which was immediately flung open, and two monks, lanterns in hand, came forward.

There was no occasion now to force the corpse into that horrible mockery of life. The monks lifted Mary from the carriage and placed her upon a stretcher; then, with a gesture, they invited the gentlemen to follow them.

The policeman shut the gates noiselessly, and Count Stockau and his brother-in-law found themselves inside a graveyard, where crosses and monuments gleamed ghostlike from the darkness as the sad cortège passed. This was the burial-ground of the Cistercian Abbey of Heiligenkreuz, and here Mary Vetsera was to find her last resting-place.

The monks entered a little building apparently used for lumber, as it was littered with all kinds of fragments of masonry, odd pieces of wood, and bricks. But a space had been cleared where stood an open coffin of common white wood.

There was no shroud in which to wrap the dead, and the beautiful young body was somewhat roughly placed inside the unlined burial-chest. Poor Mary! What an awful ending to a life which had seemed so full of promise! Rudolph lay honoured in State, but his victim's only requiem was sung by the mournful wind as it sighed among the graves - better far to have laid her uncoffined in the kindly earth than to have pushed her inside the rough box, which in itself was an outrage on decency.

Count Stockau doubled Mary's hat into a pillow, and rested the sleeper's head upon it; he then took off a gold cross which she wore round her neck, and placed the symbol of love and forgiveness between the stiff fingers.

The monks thereupon put the lid on the coffin and carried it out.

Close to the wall was an open grave. The body was consigned to it without a religious service of any description, and the earth was shovelled in upon the dead with almost feverish haste.

Mary Vetsera, whose only crime was love, was buried like a dog, and her uncles who knelt by the grave were only allowed to pray for a few seconds beside it, for the policeman tapped them on the shoulder, and told them they must not linger. They made their way back to the carriage, and reached Vienna late at night.

At 5 A.M. on the 31st of January Madame Vetsera, Hannah, and Féry left for Venice, and their place knew them no more.

I afterwards heard that my correspondence with the Baroness had been seized by the police. It was considered as strong evidence that I had been the intermediary in the intrigue between Rudolph and Mary, and the poor child's last letter to me, which was found on the bedside table at Mayerling, set the seal on my condemnation.

It was not until three weeks after Mary's death that I received this letter, the envelope of which had been opened and re-stuck. It was written in German, and ran as follows:-

192

"DEAR MARIE,

"Forgive me all the trouble I have caused. I thank you so much for everything you have done for me. If life becomes hard for you, and I fear it will after what we have done, follow us. It is the best thing you can do.

"Your

"MARY."

CHAPTER XVI
A ROYAL TRAITOR

The next morning I felt nearly distracted with grief, and at
breakfast Count Larisch said that there was nothing to keep us in
Vienna after the funeral, which was to take place that day. "I shall
leave by the Milan, Genoa, and Mentone Express early to-morrow,
but if you wish to remain a day or two longer, that is your affair,"
he informed me. George was just beginning to hear about Mary's
connection with the tragedy, but I was far too frightened to tell
him what I knew. The Count seemed glad that his bad opinion of
the family was justified, and he could not resist remarking: "You
see how right I was to warn you against the Vetseras."

I decided to make a final appeal to Aunt Cissi before I left
Vienna. I was well aware how unforgiving the Empress could be,
but I had always credited her with possessing a sense of justice,
and it came as a great shock to me when she declined to hear what
I had to say. I therefore wrote to Madame Ferenzy, who was in my
aunt's confidence, and begged her to tell the Empress that my
request for an interview arose from a wish to disclose something
very important with which I felt it my duty to acquaint her.

I received a reply from Madame Ferenzy that afternoon. The Empress absolutely refused to see me! In despair I wrote Dr. Wiederhofer and told him that I must see my aunt; would he as an old and trusted friend endeavour to persuade her to alter her decision? At four o'clock I got his answer. No, the Empress would not see me, but if I had anything to impart, she would send a trustworthy person who would communicate my information to her.

My mood was dark as the fog which enveloped the city, and the streets near the hotel were completely deserted, for most of the populace had gone to see the funeral of the Crown Prince. I was lost in my own bitter thoughts when Jenny entered, in a rather hesitating manner, with a letter which she gave me without saying a word.

The outer envelope had been addressed to my maid, and inside it was a little sealed note directed to me.

"This has just come," she said. "It was left at the hotel by a messenger."

I opened the note with no particular interest, but at the sight of the first few words I started in alarm. The letter was written in pencil, and I went over to the window in order to read it more plainly.

"If you are fearless and still faithful to your word given to the dead, bring what you know of this evening at half-past ten to the public promenade between the Schwarzenberg and the Heugasse. Be silent for the sake of his memory. R.I.U.O."

Each nerve within me tingled as I read this mysterious communication. Jenny's frightened face recalled me to myself.

"It's nothing," I said, crumpling up the letter as I spoke.

"I imagined that it might have had something to do with the poor young Baroness," replied Jenny. "You have no idea, Madame la Comtesse, of the stories which are being circulated about the tragedy. Some people say that the Crown Prince was shot by a gamekeeper; others insist that his Imperial Highness was hit on the head with a chair by the Duke of Braganza; again, it is reported that the Baroness Mary forced her way into the presence of the Crown Prince and wounded him because he wished to break off the liaison between them: indeed, they also say that she afterwards shot herself in the forest of Mayerling, where her body was discovered."

"Don't believe anything you hear," I said. "Listen, Jenny; I want some very strong tea at once, for I feel miserably ill and have a bad headache. It's imperative for me to go out this evening; don't ask any questions. I'm in no danger. I should like your cloak, and you must fetch me a one-horse cab to the servants' entrance of the hotel at a quarter to ten. Get the cab from a good distance away. I don't want to be recognised."

"Will Madame la Comtesse not allow me to go with her?" asked Jenny anxiously.

"No ..." I answered, "your place is here. Lock yourself in my room until I return, and on no account allow the Count to come in."

I then sent my maid to tell George's valet that I wished to speak to him. "The Count may return a little late," I said. "Will you say that I have gone to bed and don't wish to be disturbed, as we start so early in the morning."

I began to gather my things together – anything to distract my unwelcome thoughts. I was obstinate now, and decided that I would give Aunt Cissi's representative no information whatever. I had intended to send the steel box to the Empress, and let her do as she judged best with its contents, but I was smarting under a sense of injustice, and I resolved to be as immovable as my aunt. She should know nothing from me.

At that moment Jenny returned and handed me a card, saying as she did so, "His Excellency Count Andrássy is outside, and begs to speak with Madame la Comtesse."

I ran to the door. I was overjoyed - Count Julius Andrássy! What great good fortune had brought him to see me? He had been my best friend ever since my first arrival in Austria, and I had always confided in him whenever I found myself in a difficult position at Gödöllö.

The Count had been condemned to death in consequence of the prominent part he had taken in the Hungarian rebellion of '48, but had been pardoned, and ultimately became Chancellor of the Empire. Count Andrássy had retired from office for many years, but he was on terms of great friendship with the Emperor, and my aunt trusted him absolutely. Directly I caught sight of the kind face and honest eyes, I felt I was with a real friend, and I took both his hands in mine with a joyful exclamation.

"My poor Countess Marie," said the Count kindly, "I am so dreadfully grieved to see you under such sad circumstances, but don't lose: heart; perhaps everything will right itself."

We sat down. Then I asked, "Tell me, has my aunt relented? Oh do say that she will see me."

He shook his head. "Alas, no. Her Majesty is in such a pitiable state that it is useless to reason with her, but perhaps later ... at any rate tell me the truth. However could you have been so culpable as to become the confidante of the Crown Prince? I would never have believed it!"

I stiffened instantly. "Well, and of what am I accused? I have always loved my aunt and obeyed her wishes. Why is she so embittered without having heard my side of the story?"

"The Empress believes that you and Madame Vetsera acted together, and encouraged Rudolph's affection for Mary."

"Good Heavens!" I cried - "the thing is absurd."

"At any rate," answered the Count sternly, "it was your duty to have acquainted the Empress directly you knew what was going on."

"What could I do? My aunt herself is to blame for the result of my up-bringing. She always impressed on me that once my word was given it must never be broken, and she told me to be especially discreet over love affairs. I've only carried out her own precepts. I foolishly gave my promise to Rudolph, and I could not go from it. When I reproached him he laughed at me. Yes, Count Andrássy, I repeat, he laughed at me, and you can tell the Empress what her son said. It is not pleasant, but I will not be so misjudged. 'Since when,' Rudolph asked, 'have you been considered fit to play the saint? You are a fine one to talk to me of honour or loyalty. You who have been the go-between for my mother.'"

"Say no more, Countess."

"No, you shall listen. 'You have been the go-between for my mother since you were a girl, and yet you dare to mention morality to me, when you have not scrupled to stand by and see my father deceived.' You may well turn away your face, Count Andrássy, but I am speaking the truth. Take this message from me to my aunt. If she had been kinder to Rudolph he would have trusted her and not made use of me."

I burst into convulsive sobs, and the Count soothed me as one might a child. "Be calm. I know you feel sore and unhappy, but it will avail you nothing to preserve this attitude of resentment. Tell me, did Rudolph ever mention politics to you? Because you must know that the death of the Crown Prince is not entirely a love tragedy."

I was obstinately silent. "I've nothing to disclose," I said coldly.

"Have you nothing further to say, or will you still allow the Empress to hold you responsible for the death of her son?"

"No. I see that I am definitely prejudged, and I disdain to say more."

Count Andrássy rose from his chair. "How long do you remain in Vienna, Countess?"

"George and I leave for Italy by the first tram to-morrow."

"Don't be in such a hurry; wait a little ... It looks as if you were running away." Andrássy shook his head sadly as he uttered the last words.

"No, Count, I am not running away. We have always intended to go to the Riviera. I shall come back to Vienna in the spring for I do not fear anyone."

"Countess Marie," replied my old friend, "I wish we had been spared this interview. And I assure you that if ever you should need a friend you have one in me." He gave me a fatherly kiss, and I threw myself in his arms and cried bitterly.

"Farewell, dear child," were his last words to me.

It was our final parting, for I never saw Count Julius Andrássy again.

It was already late when I put on Jenny's cloak, and covered my fur toque with a thick veil. I carried the mysterious box under my arm, and summoned up all my courage, for I was horribly nervous. Jenny had brought the cab to the servants' entrance and, as nobody was about, I decided to slip downstairs without a moment's delay.

The night was very cold and foggy, but I was glad, as I was better able to keep my appointment unnoticed. I told the cabman to stop first at No. 5 Swartzenberg Platz, and afterwards to wait for me at the chemist's shop at the corner of the Ring. My knees trembled as I alighted and I grasped the precious box convulsively. I crossed the bridge, and on my right found the little tree-bordered promenade where Rudolph's representative had asked me to meet him.

It was a gloomy place, quite deserted at that hour of night. A tall lamp shed its watery rays through the mist, but I felt more secure near the light, and I waited for what seemed an interminable time. All at once I heard short sharp footsteps, and saw a man coming up to where I stood. He wore a Steiermack-Mantel and a felt hat, and I suddenly became frightened and tried to pass him.

The stranger looked at me, and slightly raised his hat.

"Countess Larisch?" he asked quietly.

"What do you want?" I stammered, still moving on.

My interlocutor took a step forward and whispered, "*Rudolph.*"

I stopped instantly. "You have received my letter?" inquired the stranger.

"Yes, I have received a letter. But that is not all."

"Ah. ... I understand. R.I.U.O."

I at once produced the box and offered it to the stranger, but he did not take it.

"I should like a few words with you, Countess Larisch," said the unknown. "I think you are a brave woman to come here - but we must not converse under the light." He walked slowly away, and I followed him. I was no longer afraid, for the low voice of the stranger was so beautiful, and his whole bearing so dignified that I knew he was no ordinary person.

"Thank you for coming," he went on, "it is right to fulfil a last wish."

"But," I said, "there was nothing else to do." I had promised to give the box to the person who could prove his right to demand it."

"Have you ever spoken of this trust?"

"Never - *never.*"

The stranger seemed greatly relieved at my words.

"Did 'he' tell you what this mystery was about?"

"No, I am quite in ignorance."

"Well, well, it is better that such is the case, otherwise your life might be forfeited."

"Please - please take the box," I interrupted, for I was anxious to get away.

Two hands came from under the stranger's cloak and took the box from me, and I shall never forget their look of strength. On one little finger sparkled a great diamond, and when I touched those wonderful hands I suddenly felt very calm for I knew that I had given the box to the right person.

"Countess Marie," said the stranger, "I should like to do something for you. Rudolph treated you in a most shameful way. I know all about it, and consider it a mean action on his part to have involved you in his affairs."

I looked at him gratefully.

"I suppose you have no idea who I am, Countess?"

"None," I replied.

He took off his hat and stared me full in the face, while I started back in astonishment.

"Imperial Highness!" I ejaculated. The stranger was the Archduke John of Tuscany!

I had only met the Archduke occasionally in society, but I instantly recognised his extraordinary eyes and interesting face, and I remembered the close friendship which had existed between him and the Crown Prince. I had also heard that the Archduke was on bad terms with the Emperor, and that there was a likelihood of his leaving Austria at no distant date.

"Don't be alarmed, Countess," remarked the Archduke cynically and sadly, "I'm not dangerous." Then he asked me how long I had had the box in my possession.

"About a fortnight," I replied.

"Did you never attempt to open it after the tragedy?"

"No - it's quite untouched."

"Well, I was afraid lest you might be tempted to give it to the Empress, and I only discovered this morning where you were stopping."

I told him all about Count Andrássy's visit.

"Oh, did she send that old 'musk-deer' to see you?" He laughed as he spoke, and then said more seriously, "But you would have done well for yourself if you had given this box to the Count, for I assure you that instead of being forbidden the Hofburg you would have been made a Duchess. Never mind, things have happened for the best; you could not save a coward like Rudolph, but you've saved my life."

I began to cry; it was all so uncanny and mysterious. The Archduke took my hand.

"Don't regret Rudolph," he said; "if the Emperor had found these papers, matters would have been infinitely worse. The Crown Prince has killed himself, but if the Emperor had known all, it would have been his duty to have had him tried by military law, and shot as a traitor."

"Oh, my God!" I cried. "What did he do? Was he thinking of the Crown of Hungary?"

The Archduke nodded assentingly, and I suddenly thought of my aunt's words long ago, when she told me that Rudolph was in the hands of the Freemasons; but Elizabeth had little reason to object, as she herself was always coquetting with the Socialist party.

"Do you think that Rudolph's plans miscarried," I asked, "and that he received information to this effect whilst he was at Mayerling? ... He was afraid of something," I continued, "for, besides having given me this box, I am told that he sent most of his papers some weeks ago to M. de Szoggenzi-Marisch."

The Archduke was silent. "It may be," he answered evasively. "But do you understand what the fear of discovery must have meant to Rudolph, with his nervous constitution undermined by drugs and brandy? Fear alone might have made him commit suicide. It is a pity he was so weak. He broke his word to me, and I trusted him. But a bottle of brandy seems to have turned him into a contemptible coward. However, we must not stand here any longer; there are police spies all over Vienna. Good-bye, Countess Marie; you may never see me again, but I shall always remember what you have done for me."

I was greatly puzzled. "Imperial Highness," I asked, "are you going away from Austria?"

He smiled. "Yes. I'm going to die without dying, for I am tired of the hollow things of life, and I intend to begin a new career ... and now farewell. Don't forget me."

He kissed my hand, and was gone.

I watched John of Tuscany as he passed into the fog and disappeared in the gloom of the night. And, when I read later that he had been drowned at sea, I thought of that evening in Vienna when he bade me farewell. Has he died without dying? I think so. And I believe that the Archduke, despite all evidence to the contrary, will return in his own good time.

I got back to the hotel unobserved, and the next morning at five o'clock we left Vienna for the Riviera.

I made a clean breast of everything to my husband, and to his eternal credit he behaved like a white man through and through. He believed my word, and placed himself entirely on my side, and he never once wavered during the storm of gossip and scandal which assailed me.

I disdained to reply to my calumniators, although Alexandre Baltazzi, who adored Mary, denounced me as having contributed to her downfall. I could have shown him his niece's letters from

Cairo, which would have afforded proof positive that she was not sinless when she first met Rudolph, but I let it all pass unnoticed.

I never saw the Emperor and the Empress again, and on no occasion did I ever endeavour to do so. We spent the early spring on the Riviera, and stayed at Vienna on our way back to Pardubitz. Life went on much in the usual way. Each year I spent the summer at Tegernsee and the autumn at Vienna. Everyone was quite nice to me; my friends remained my friends, and my father and mother treated me as if nothing had happened.

Count Larisch and I lived together until 1896, when our marriage was legally annulled, but the proceedings had nothing whatever to do with the tragedy of Mayerling, as has been stated by certain imaginative writers.

It is incredible that the public should usually be so ready to believe what it sees in print, and the inaccuracy of those journalists and bookmakers who have considered themselves competent to write about events in my life is amazing. I read lately a highly descriptive account of Rudolph's first meeting with Mary at my palace in Vienna, with the usual melodramatic background of shaded red lights and palms, and if I remember rightly the Prince was supposed to discover her, like the Sleeping Beauty, on a couch. There is a Larisch Palace certainly, but it did not belong to my husband, and I usually stopped at a hotel.

It has also been asserted that I was given money by Rudolph for having assisted him to meet Mary, and that my terrible extravagance at last exhausted my aunt's generosity. I never received a dowry or any large sums of money from the Empress. It is true that she gave me many beautiful presents, and that my trousseau was a joint gift from her and the Emperor, but that is about the extent of what I received from them; and as for the assertion that Rudolph lent or gave me money, I can only characterise it as ridiculous. The statement that a letter from me to the Crown Prince was found after his death in the breast pocket of a dolman is, however, accurate, but the money alluded to in the note concerned Mary and not me.

Far too much secrecy has hitherto been preserved about the tragedy at Mayerling, and the mystery arose because every one in authority at first completely lost his head. The proper course would have been to tell the truth immediately about the death of the Crown Prince. It would doubtless have been a ninety-nine days' wonder but it would not have been actively remembered. Rudolph never had a reputation for morality and little was expected of him. The Emperor has only himself to blame for the reports which have increased as time goes on. It has been asserted that Rudolph was Mary's brother, and that, driven mad by the discovery, he murdered her and afterwards committed suicide. There certainly was some gossip about Mary's parentage, but it never concerned the Emperor or any princes of the Imperial House.

The story which has found most credence in circles which count is that Rudolph fell a victim to Mary's uncle, who avenged his niece's dishonour. My narrative disproves this; the last thing which the Baltazzis desired was any kind of scandal, and the thought of murder never entered their minds. The shattered condition of the Crown Prince's head gave rise to the rumour that it was smashed in by the butt end of a gun, but the unimpeachable testimony of Dr. Wiederhofer, who saw the body and dressed the wounds, proves this to be untrue.

What actually happened during the time that Mary and Rudolph were alone at Mayerling is entirely a matter for conjecture. There is not the slightest doubt that the Prince anticipated a crisis of some sort, and it is unquestionable that he and the Archduke John had planned a *coup d'état* together. Something transpired to make Rudolph afraid of the consequences should his plans be discovered, and rightly or wrongly he miscalculated the extent of his father's displeasure. He may have felt that flight or a return to Vienna was equally impossible, and, rendered desperate through fear, inflamed by brandy, he made up his mind to kill himself. In my opinion the worst that could have happened to the Crown Prince, had it been discovered he was plotting for the throne of Hungary, would have been incarceration "owing to unsound mind."

Count Andrássy said plainly that something beyond a love drama was responsible for the tragedy; the Archduke John corroborated this statement, and the affair of the steel box makes me absolutely certain of it.

The world may well wonder why Rudolph, the heir-apparent to the thrones of Austria and Hungary, should have involved himself in the schemes of men who were striving for the separation of Hungary from Austria.

Was the Prince tired of waiting to be king, and did some subtle brain assume that the Emperor, when the crisis came, would shrink from the horror of a conflict with his son, and that the independence of Hungary would be achieved without the firing of a shot?

I cannot tell, and I doubt if the time will ever come when Rudolph's motives will be revealed.

Twenty-four years have passed since that day when the Empress refused to see me, and judged me unheard. Time has softened the bitterness which I once felt, and, looking back, I can see that my aunt was not wholly unreasonable in what she did. Perhaps I should have acted in the same manner, under the same circumstances, but it was hard for me to pass out of the life of one whom I loved so well, and whose confidence I had unfalteringly respected. ... This is all I have to say.

GENEALOGICAL TABLE

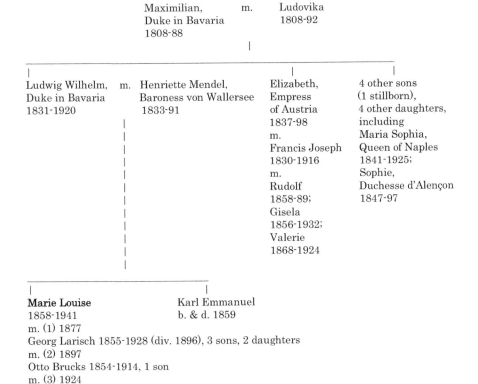

Maximilian,   m.   Ludovika
Duke in Bavaria   1808-92
1808-88

Ludwig Wilhelm, m.	Henriette Mendel,	Elizabeth,	4 other sons
Duke in Bavaria	Baroness von Wallersee	Empress	(1 stillborn),
1831-1920	1833-91	of Austria	4 other daughters,
		1837-98	including
		m.	Maria Sophia,
		Francis Joseph	Queen of Naples
		1830-1916	1841-1925;
		m.	Sophie,
		Rudolf	Duchesse d'Alençon
		1858-89;	1847-97
		Gisela	
		1856-1932;	
		Valerie	
		1868-1924	

Marie Louise   Karl Emmanuel
1858-1941   b. & d. 1859
m. (1) 1877
Georg Larisch 1855-1928 (div. 1896), 3 sons, 2 daughters
m. (2) 1897
Otto Brucks 1854-1914, 1 son
m. (3) 1924
William H. Meyers 1859-? (div. 1928), no issue

Also available in this series

Life of Alexander II, F.E. Grahame

Alexander III, Tsar of Russia, Charles Lowe

The Intimate Life of the Last Tsarina, Princess Catherine Radziwill

Collected Works: Once a Grand Duke, Always a Grand Duke, Twilight of Royalty, Alexander, Grand Duke of Russia

Frederick, Crown Prince and Emperor, Rennell Rodd

Letters of the Empress Frederick, edited by Sir Frederick Ponsonby

Between two Emperors: The Willy-Nicky Telegrams and Letters, 1894-1914

Potsdam Princes, Ethel Howard

Richard III, Sir Clements Markham

The Complete Works: The Journal of a Disappointed Man; A Last Diary; Enjoying Life and other Literary Remains, W.N.P. Barbellion